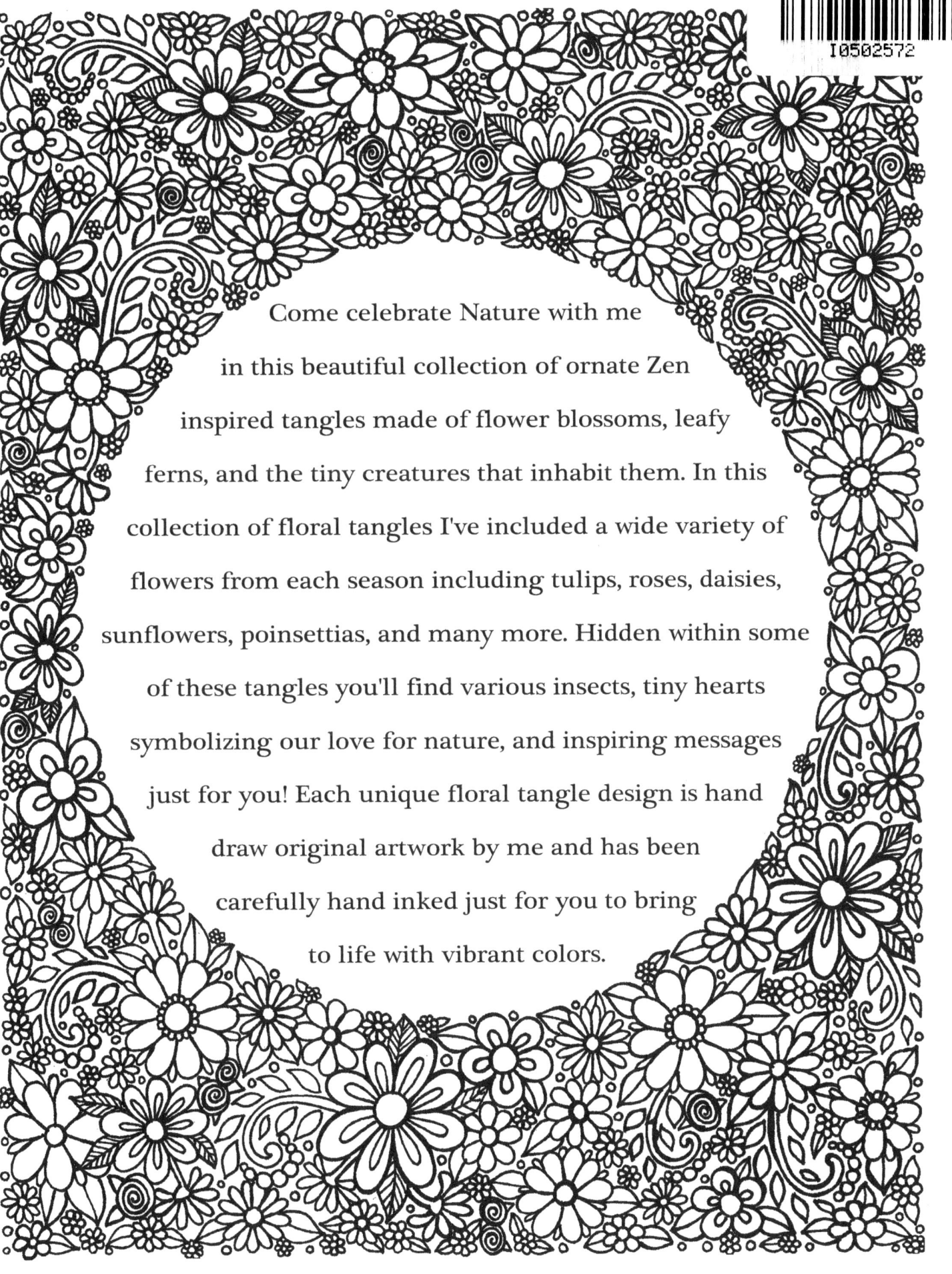

Come celebrate Nature with me
in this beautiful collection of ornate Zen
inspired tangles made of flower blossoms, leafy
ferns, and the tiny creatures that inhabit them. In this
collection of floral tangles I've included a wide variety of
flowers from each season including tulips, roses, daisies,
sunflowers, poinsettias, and many more. Hidden within some
of these tangles you'll find various insects, tiny hearts
symbolizing our love for nature, and inspiring messages
just for you! Each unique floral tangle design is hand
draw original artwork by me and has been
carefully hand inked just for you to bring
to life with vibrant colors.

This book belongs to:

....

Coloring Tips for Blossoms and Bugs

- Use the Color Test Page provided in the back of the book to test color blending with colored pencils and ink flow with gel pens.

- Don't stress if you get outside the lines. Sometimes the greatest masterpieces start out as mishaps! So enjoy yourself!

- Colored pencils are the most widely used and versatile medium to use for the blending of colors together and also for application and ease of use when coloring, especially for small details.

- Please feel free to share your work in progress pics and finished masterpieces with friends and family on social media with the hashtag #BlossomsAndBugs or you can link it by using #OfficeInkDesigns to my Artist Page.

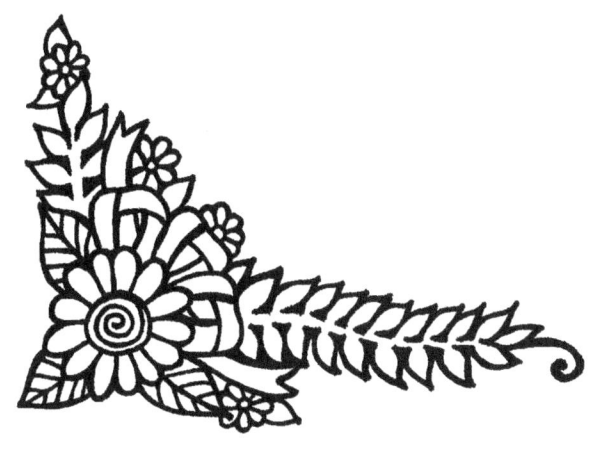
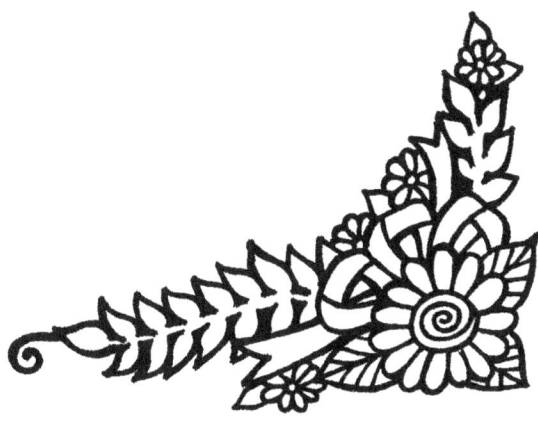

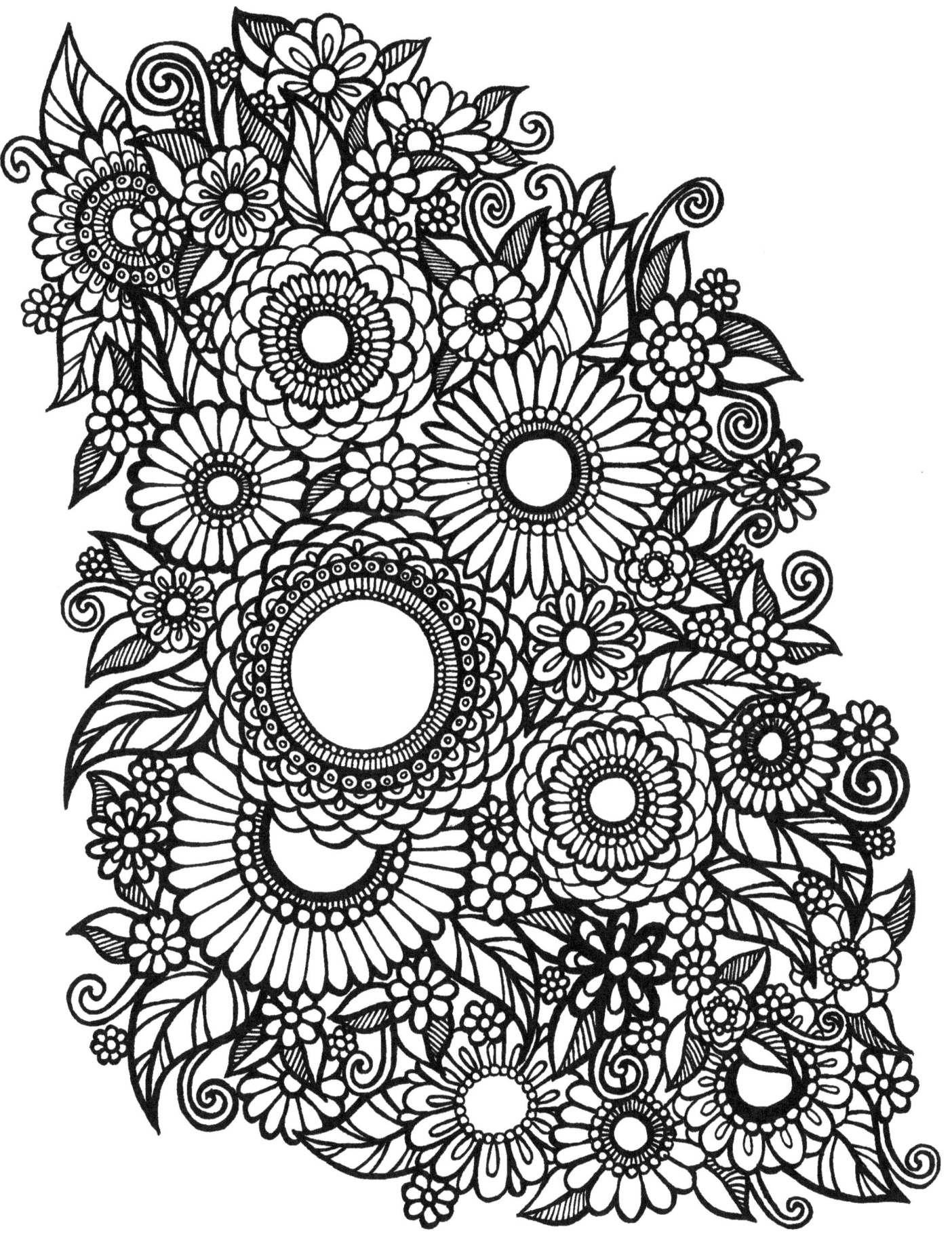

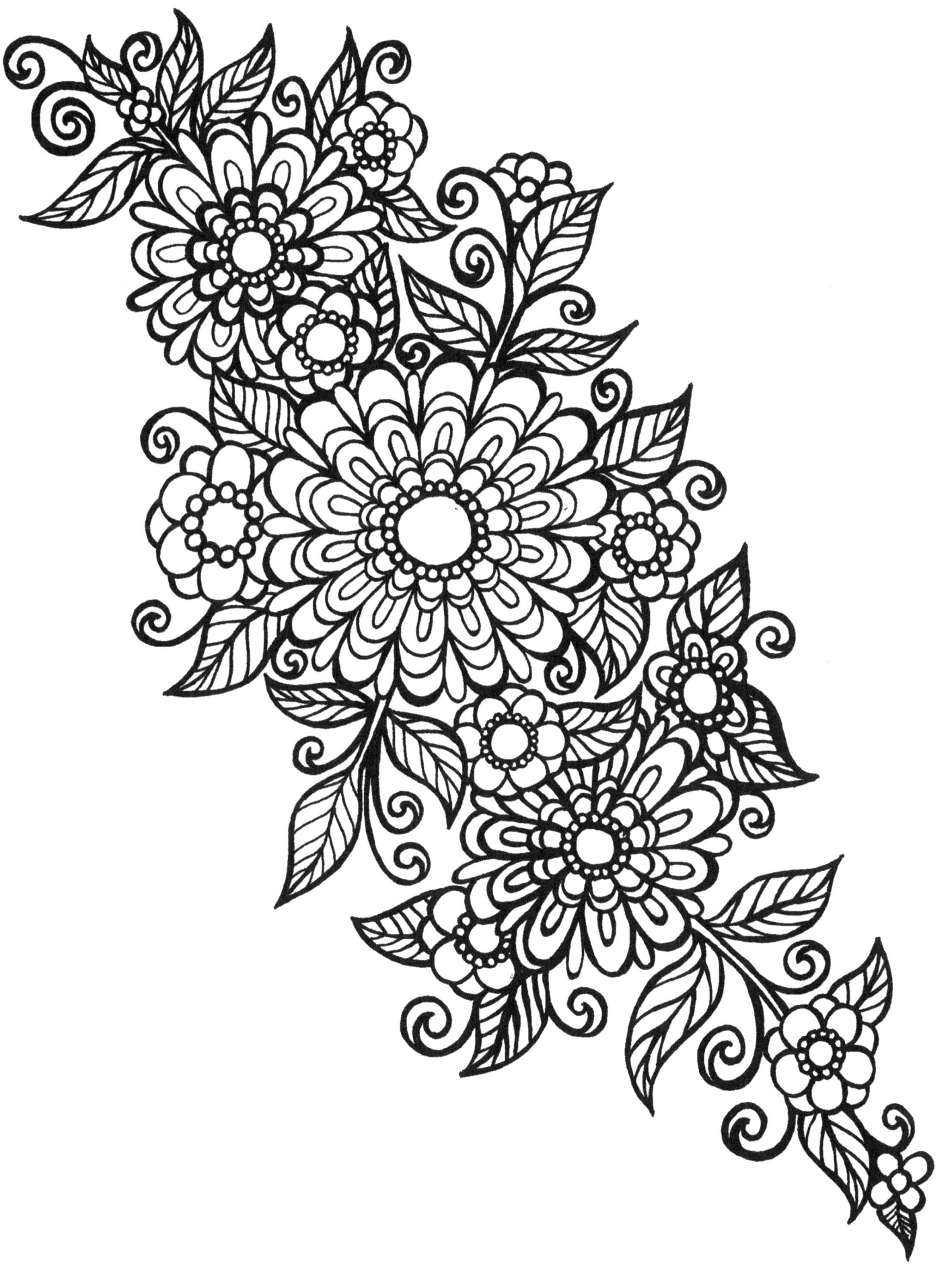

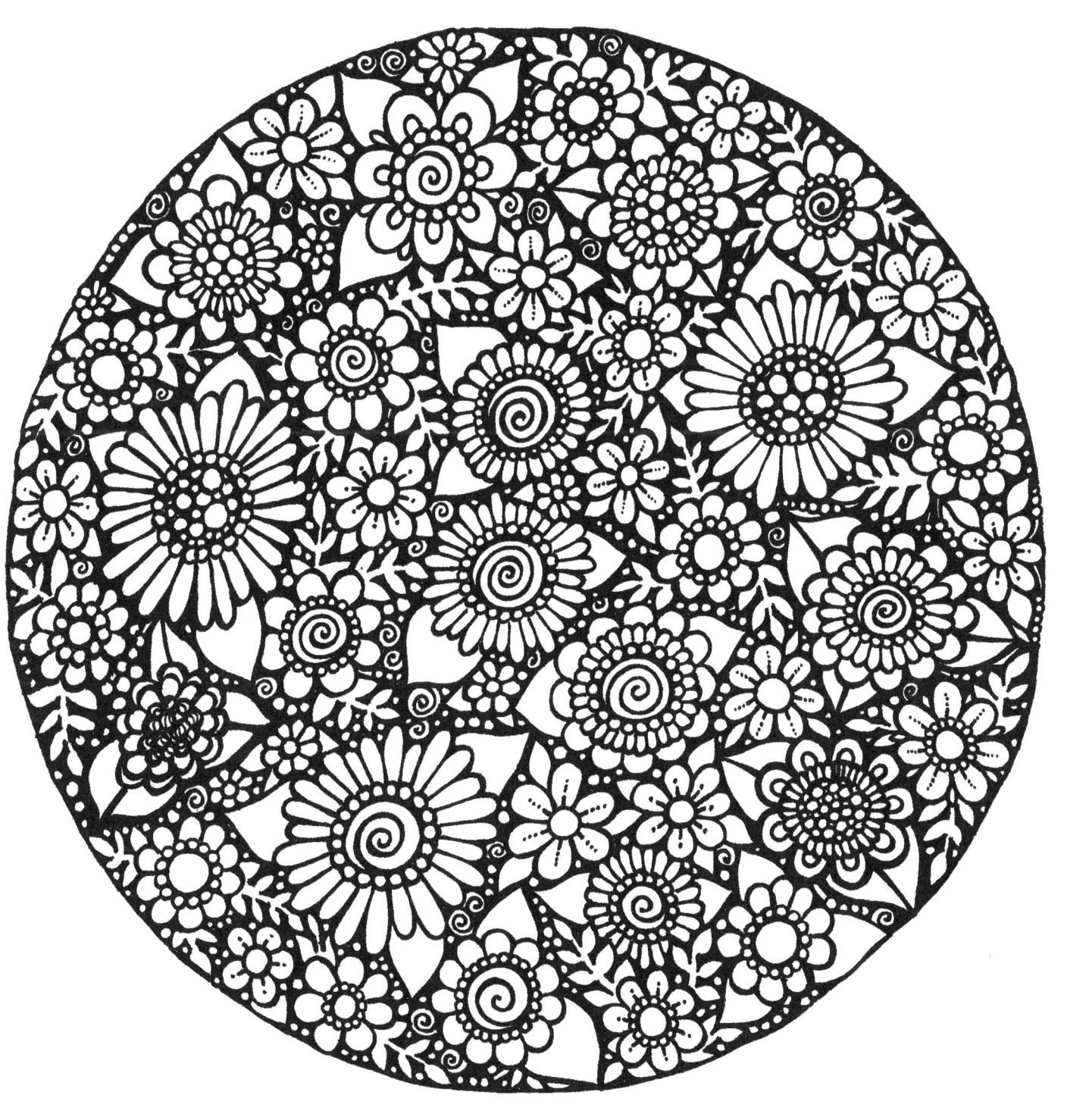

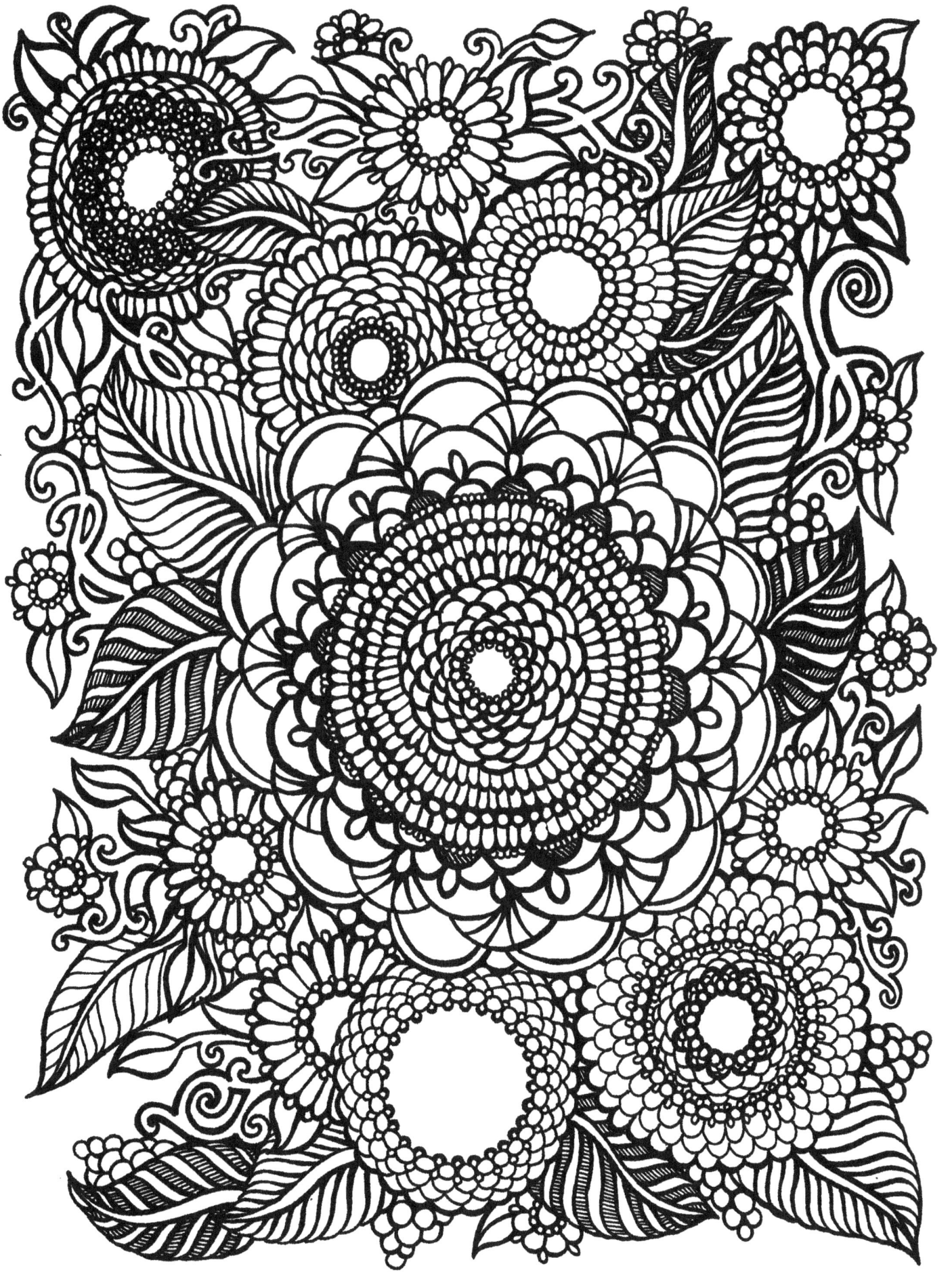

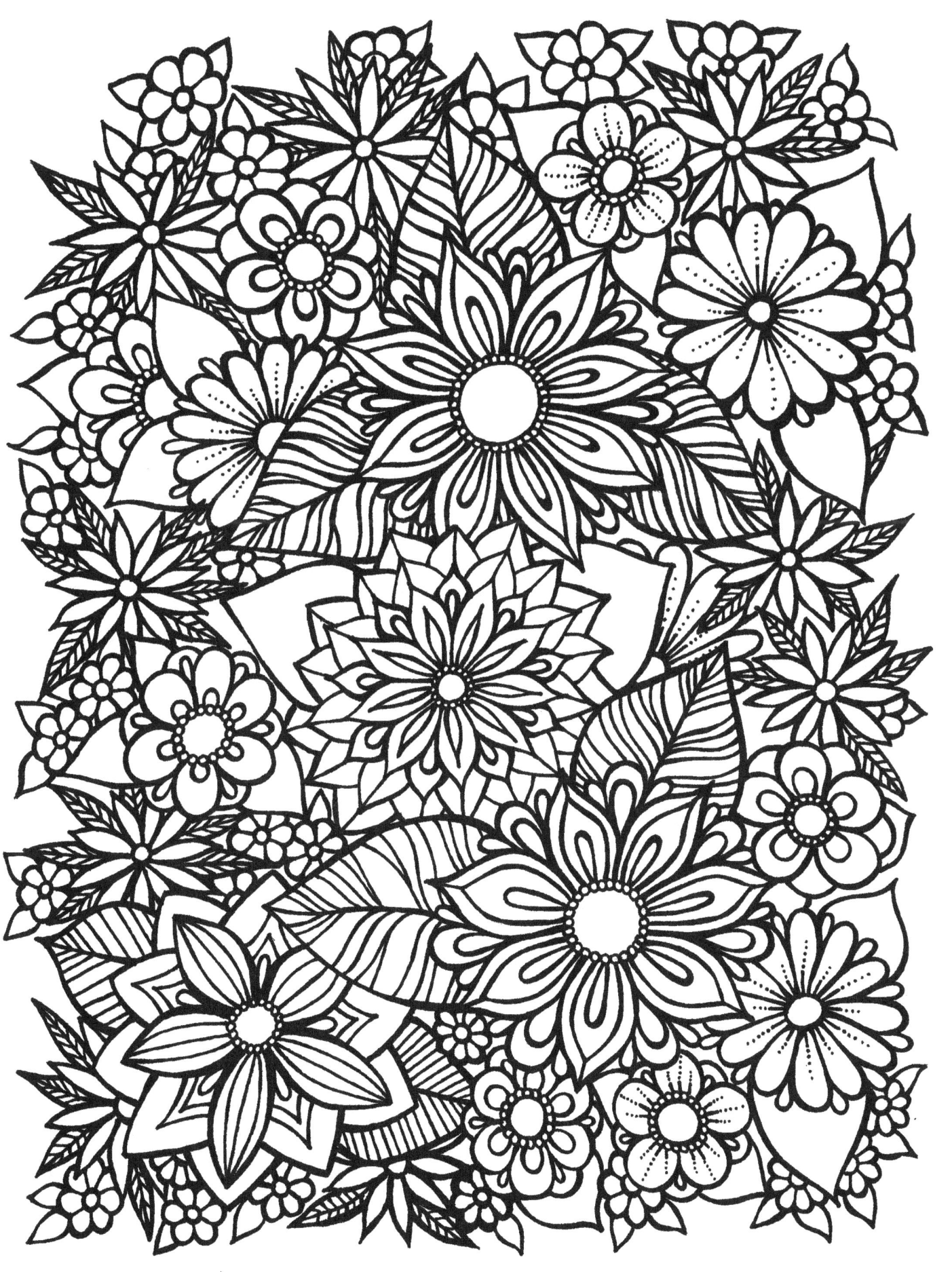

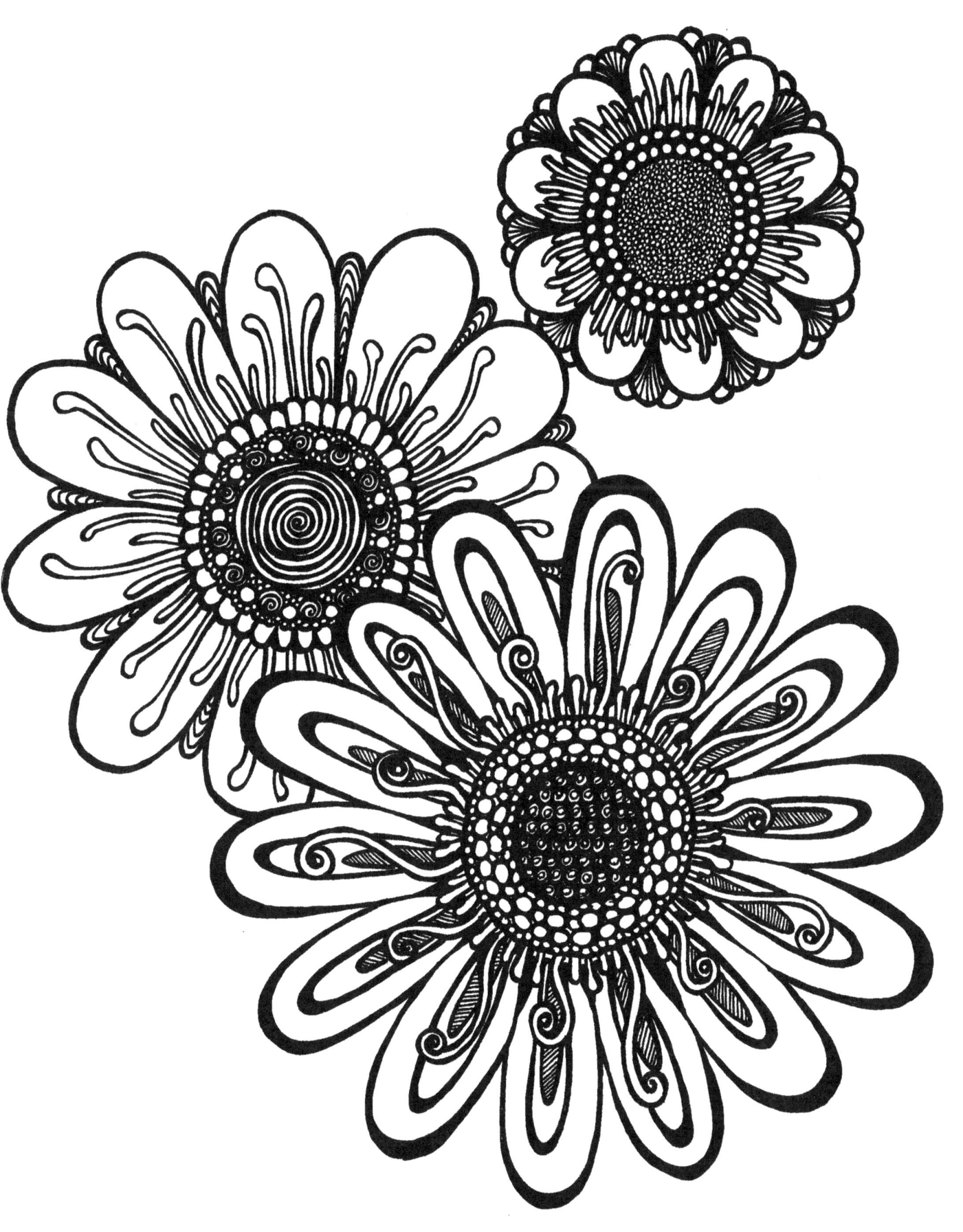

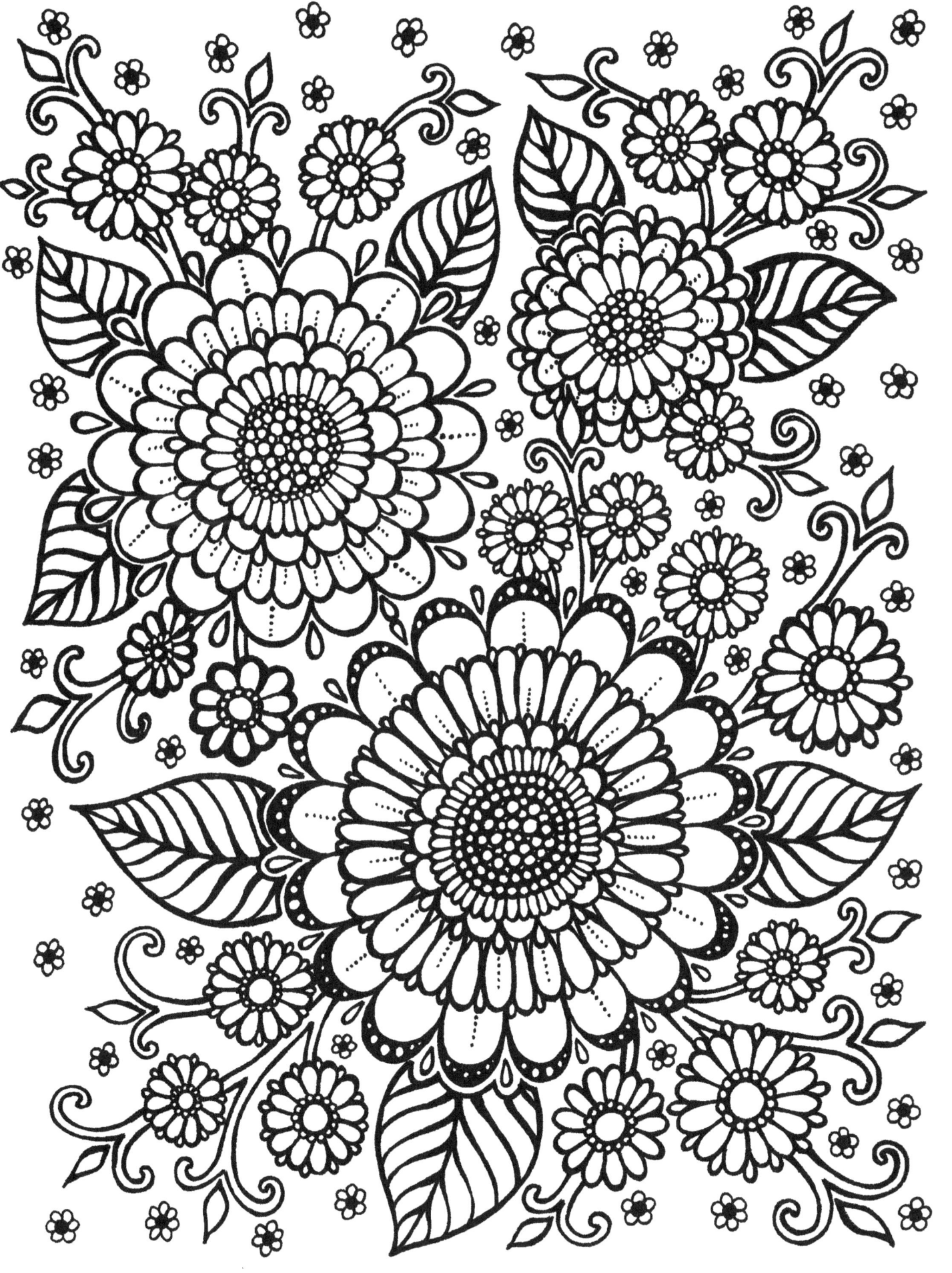

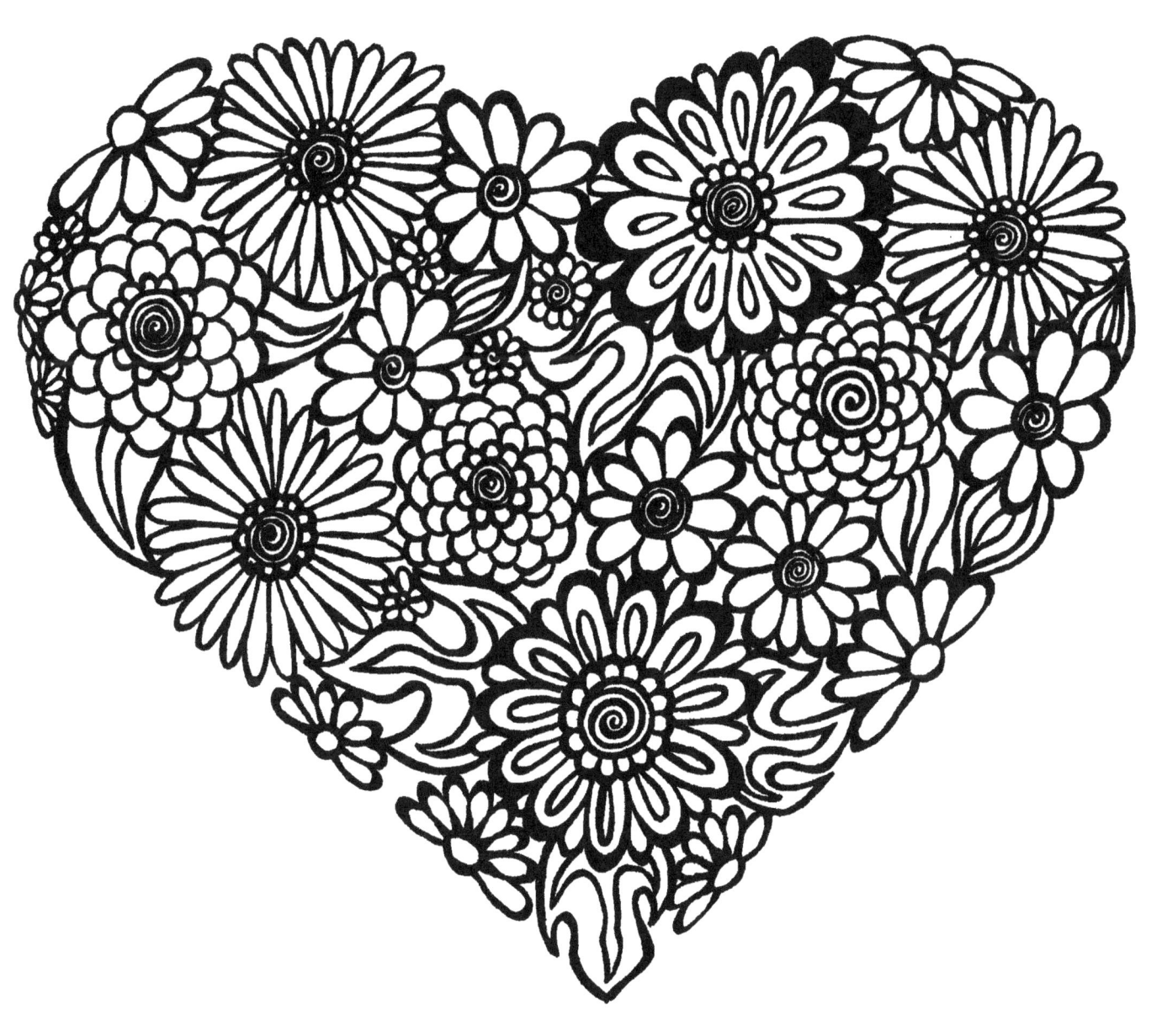

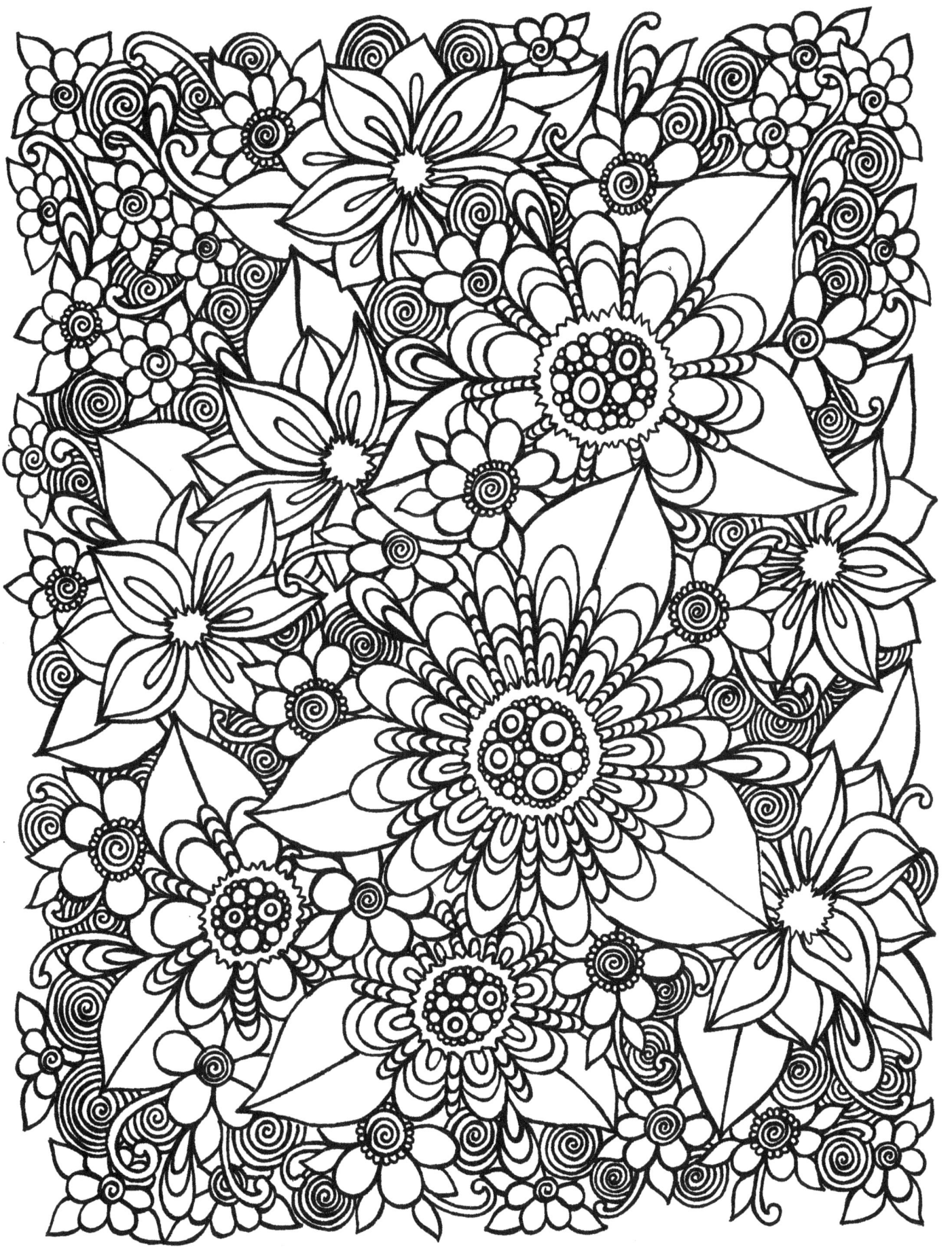

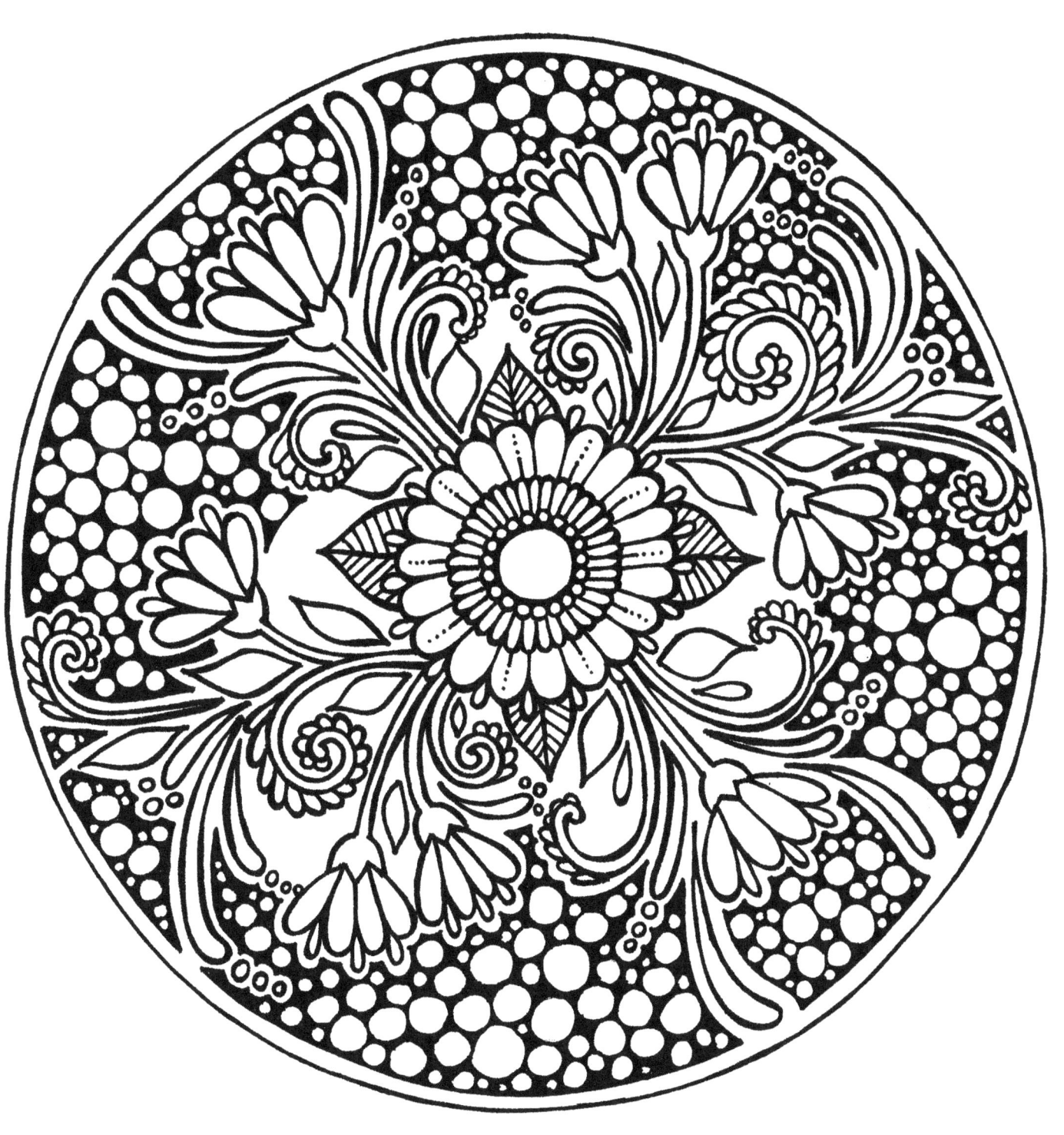

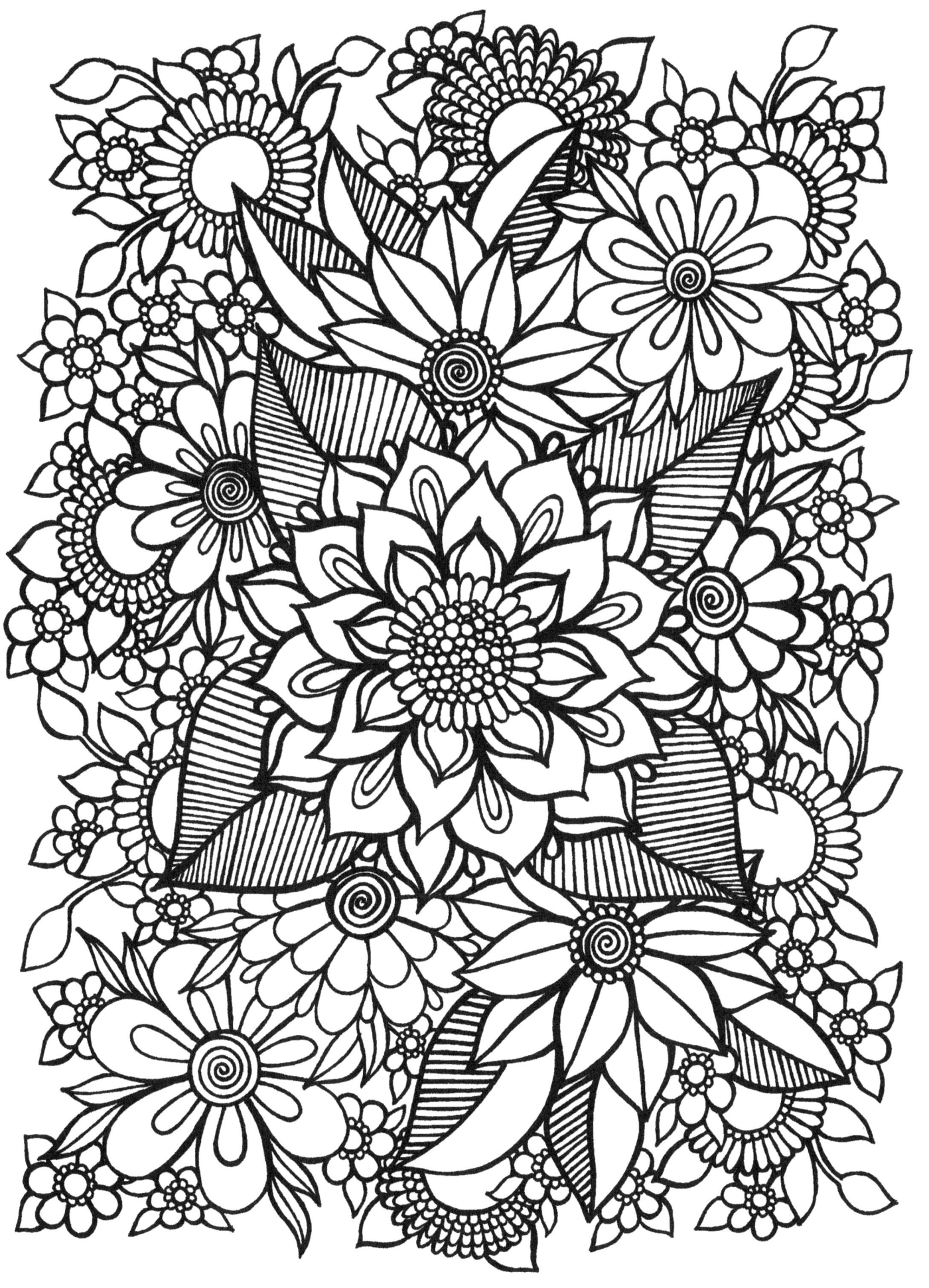

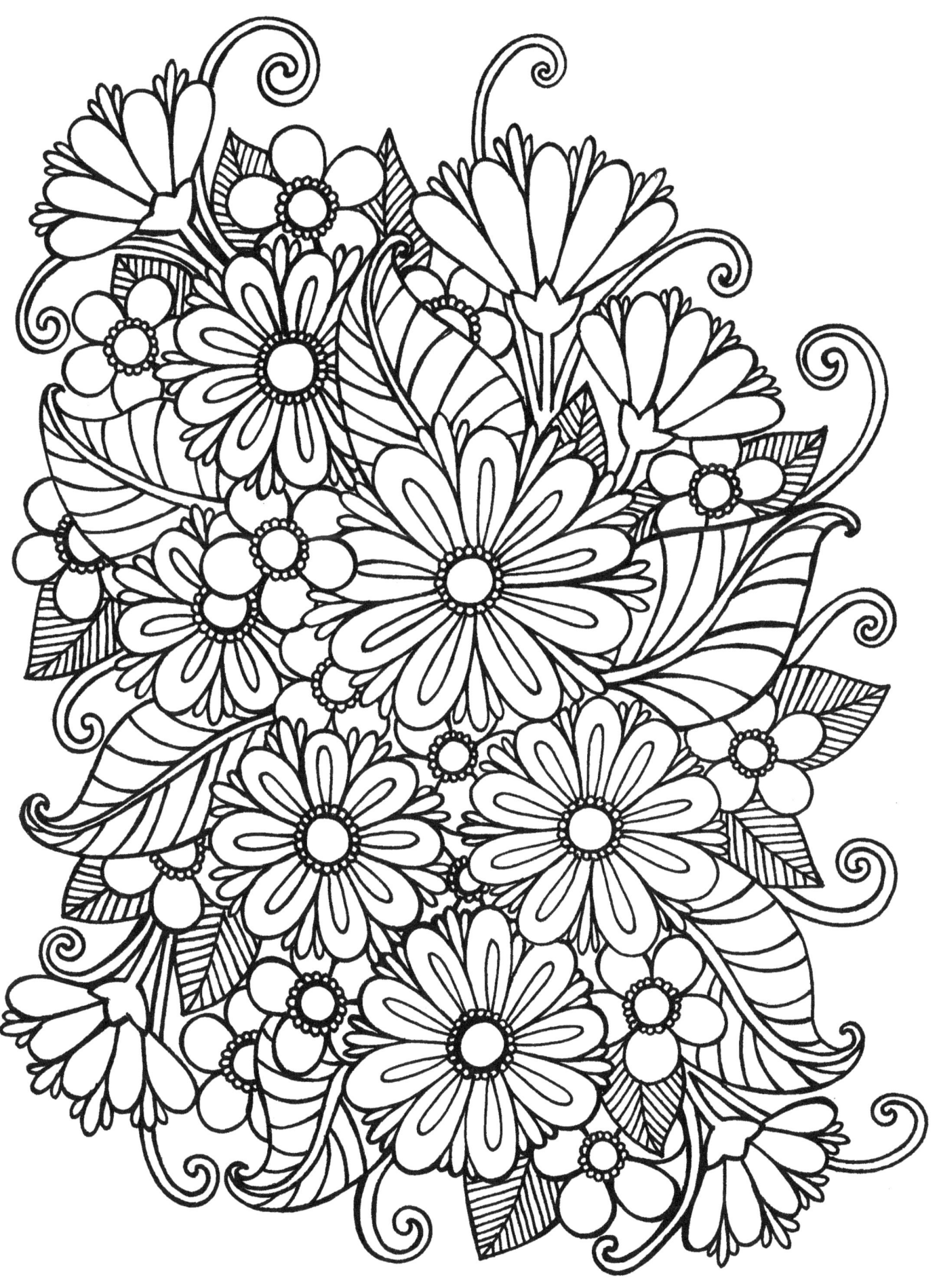

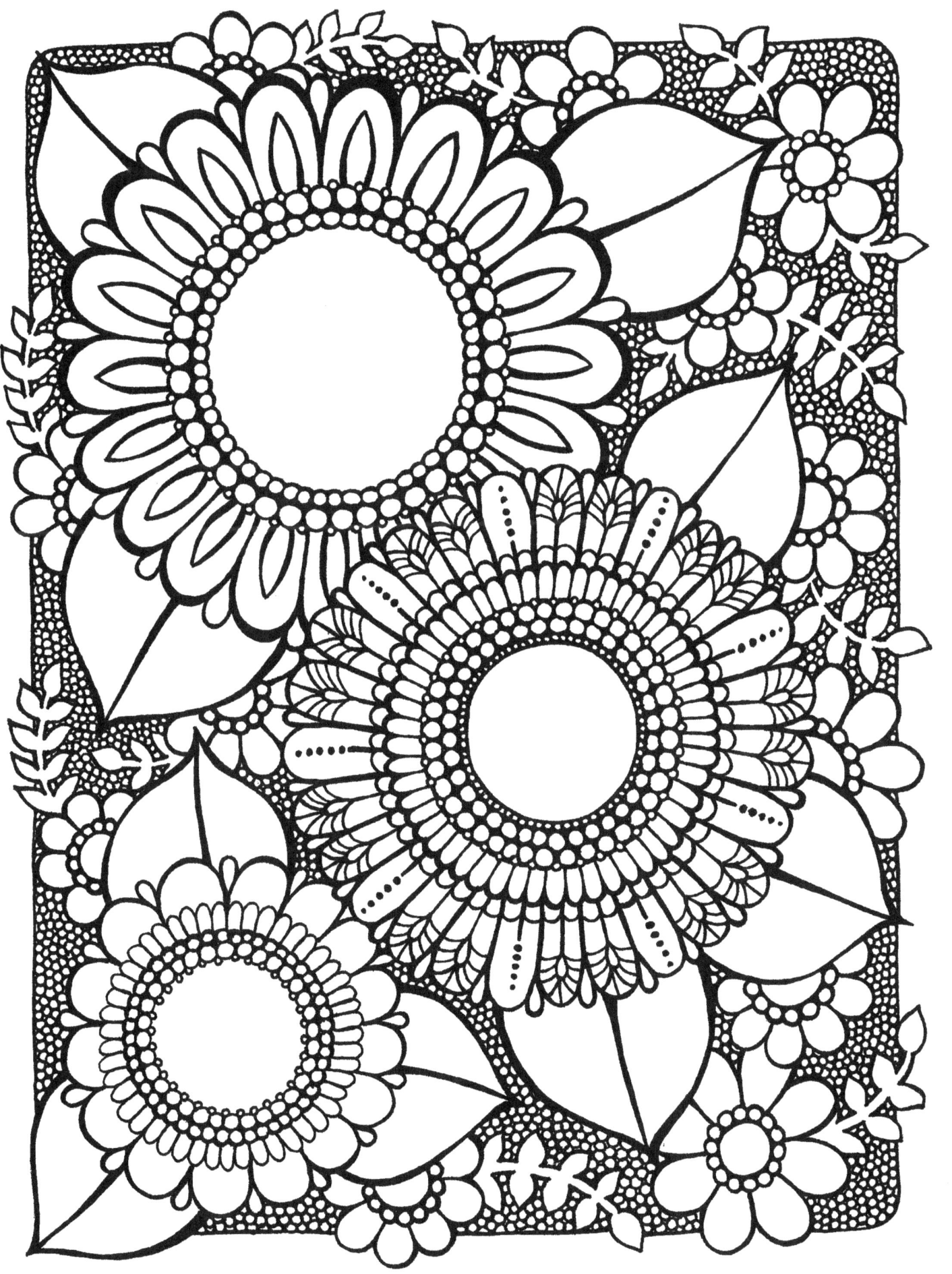

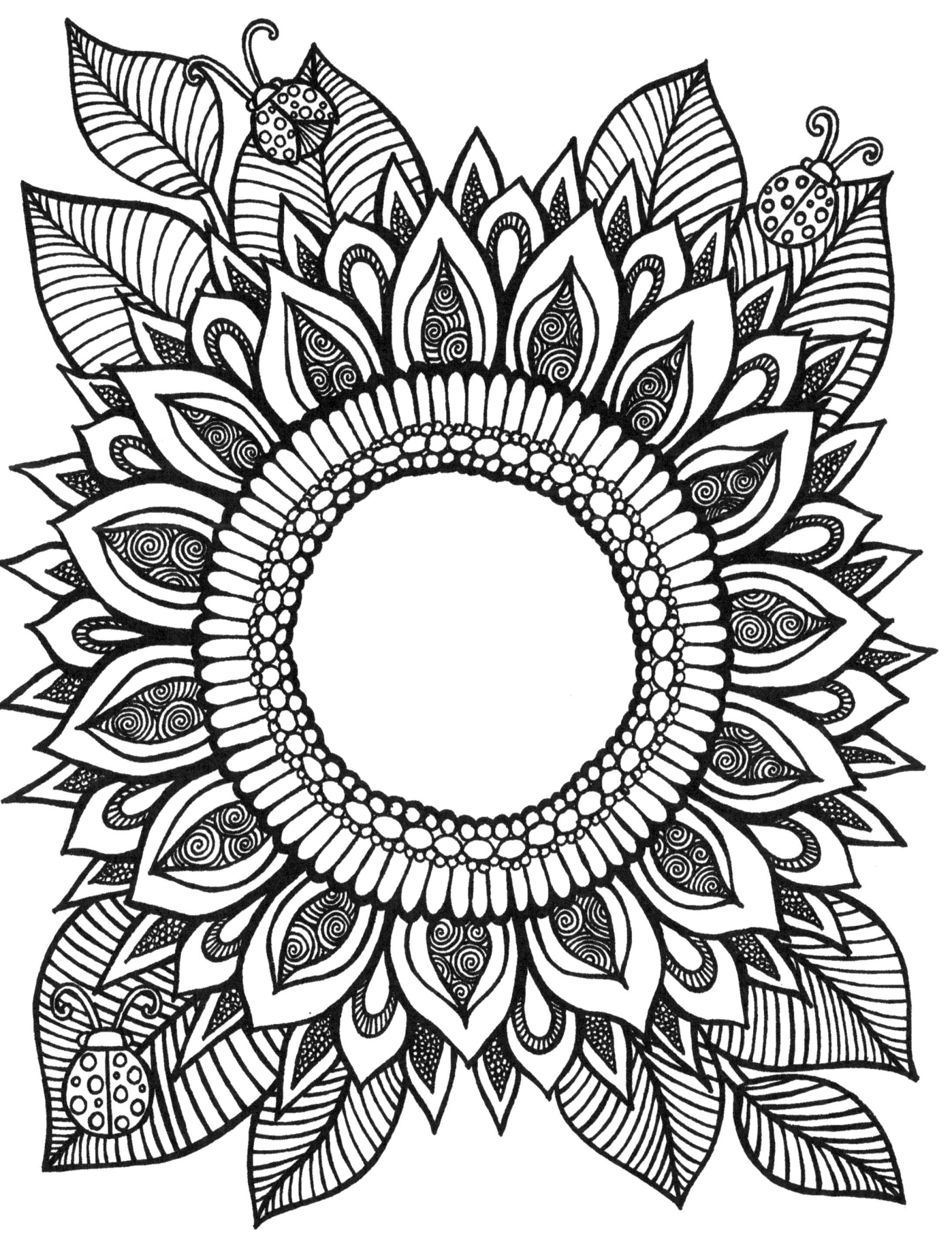

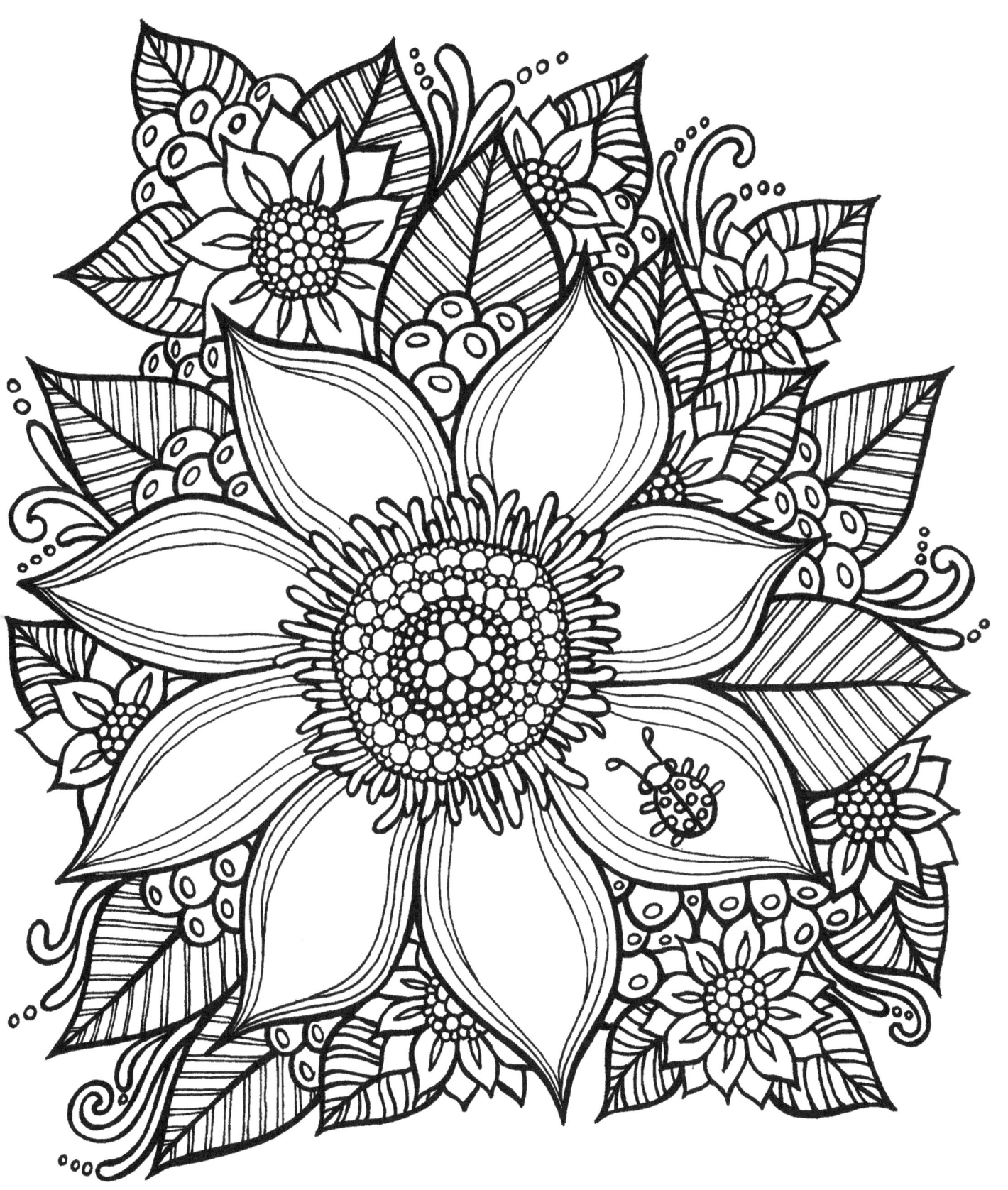

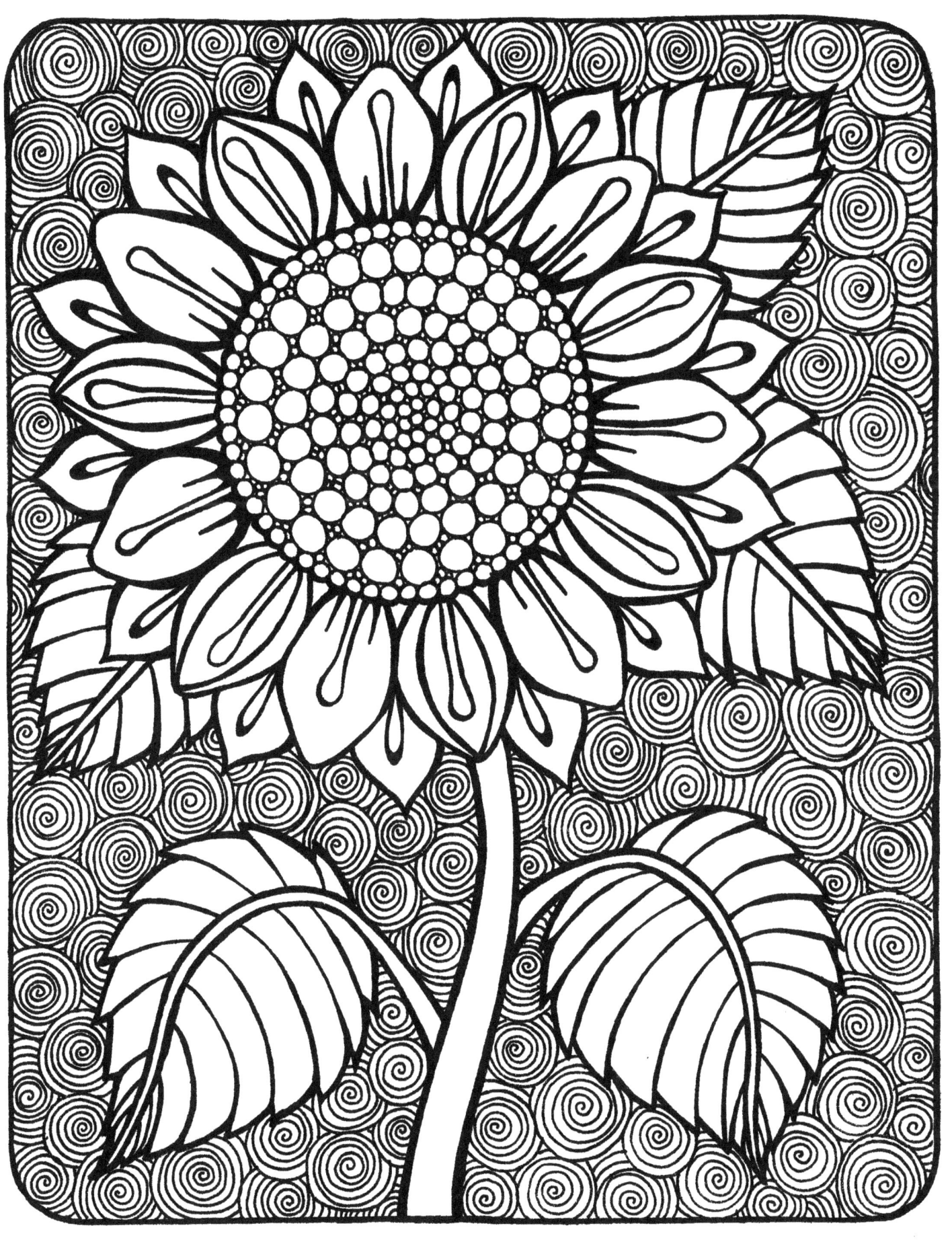

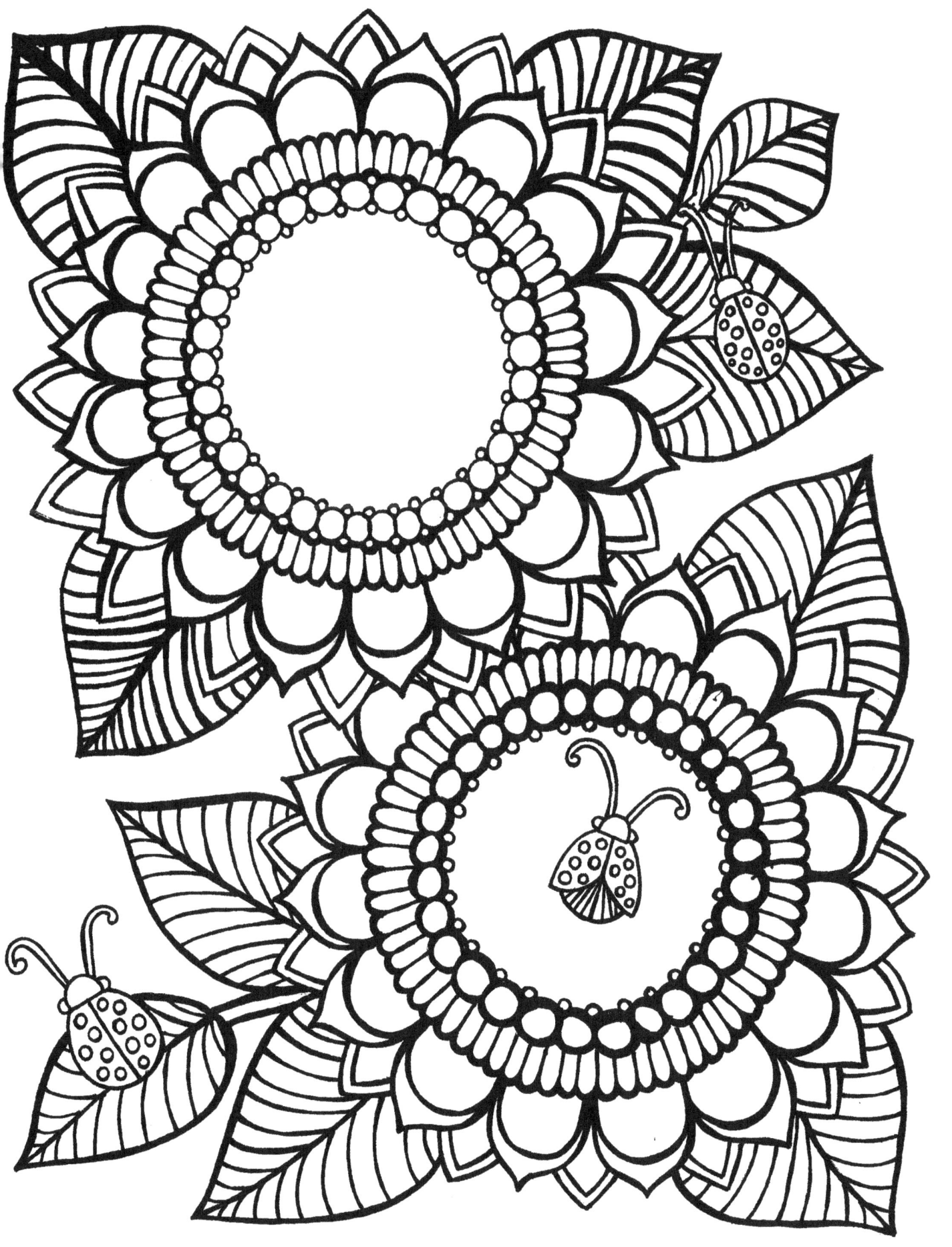

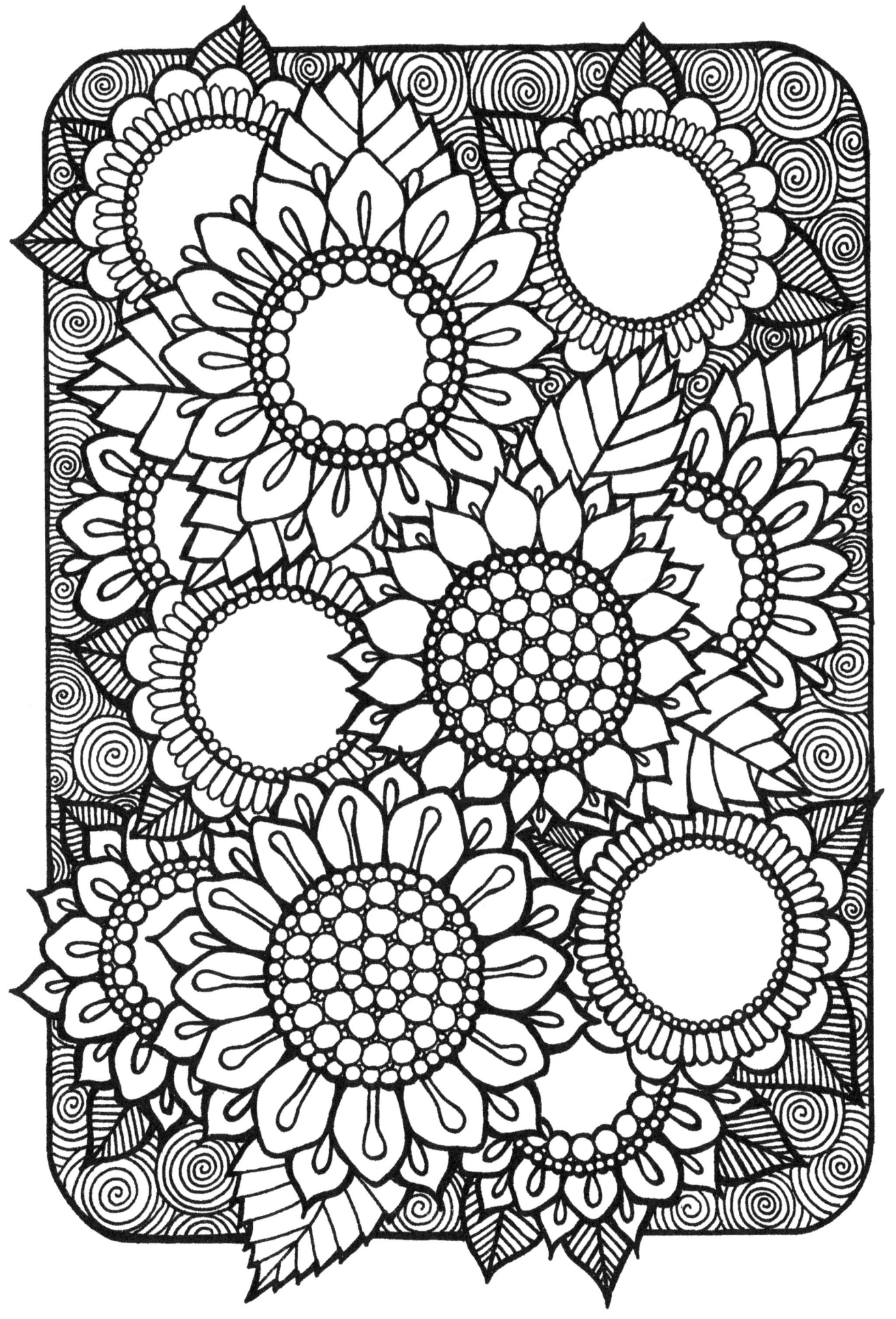

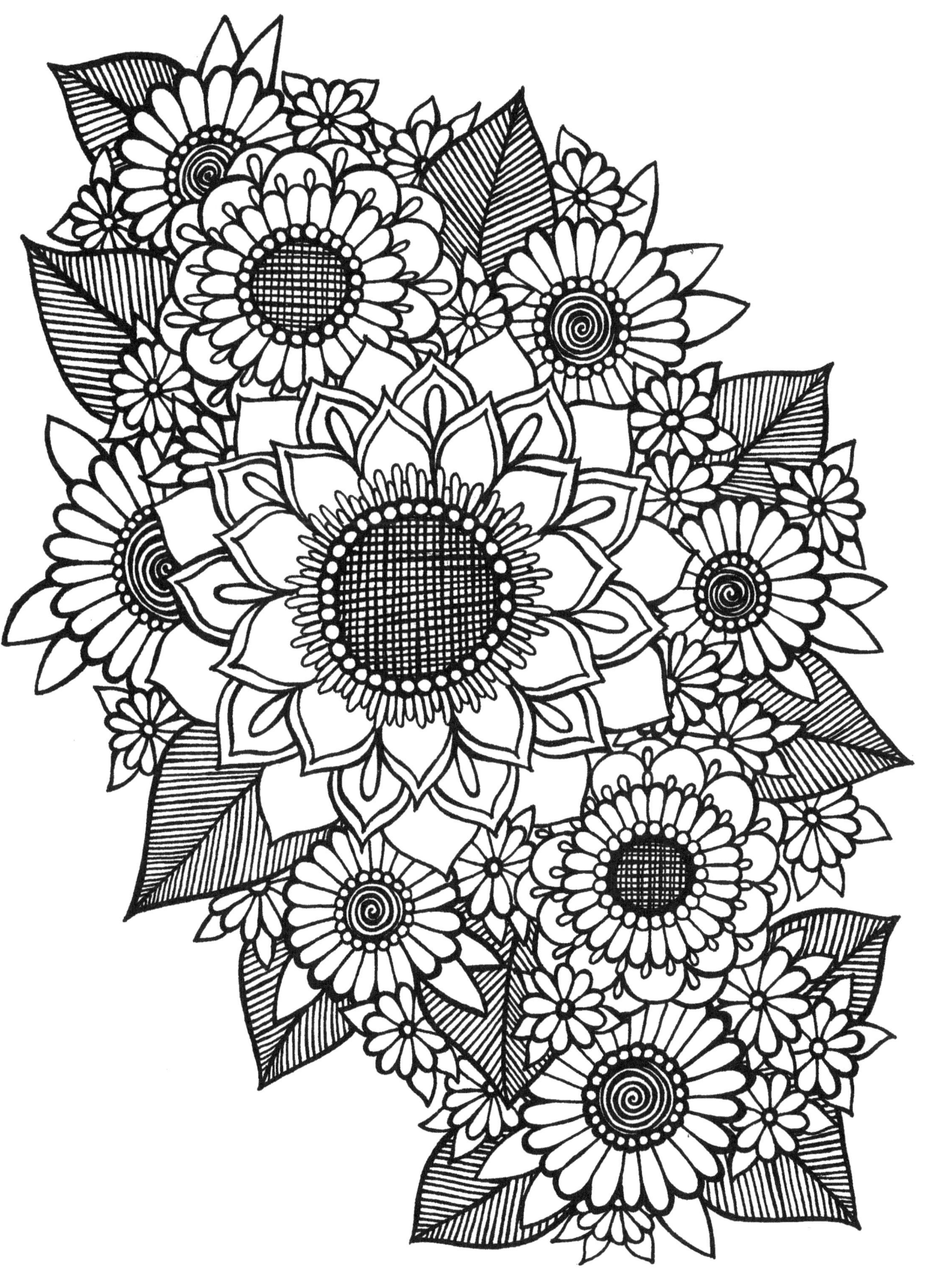

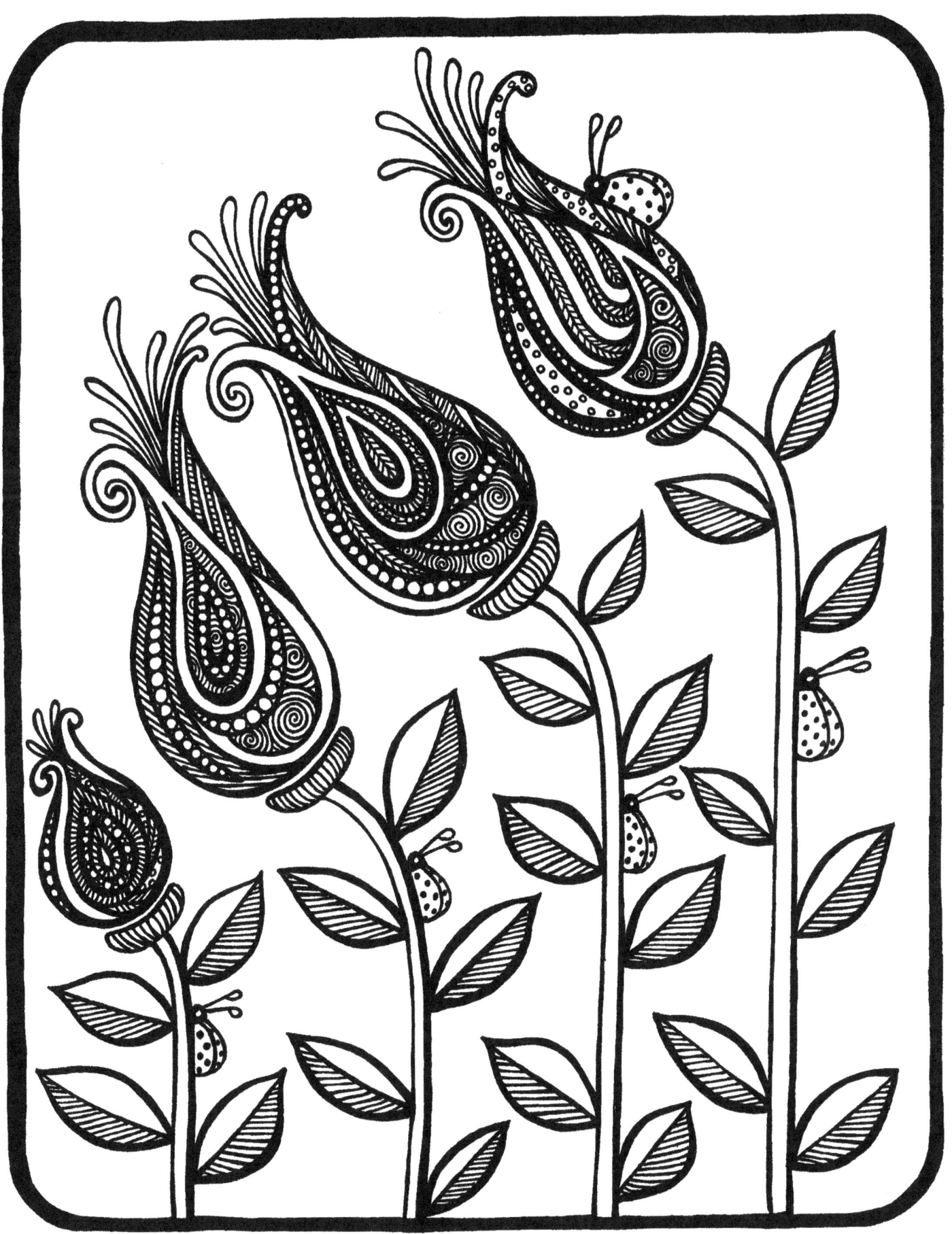

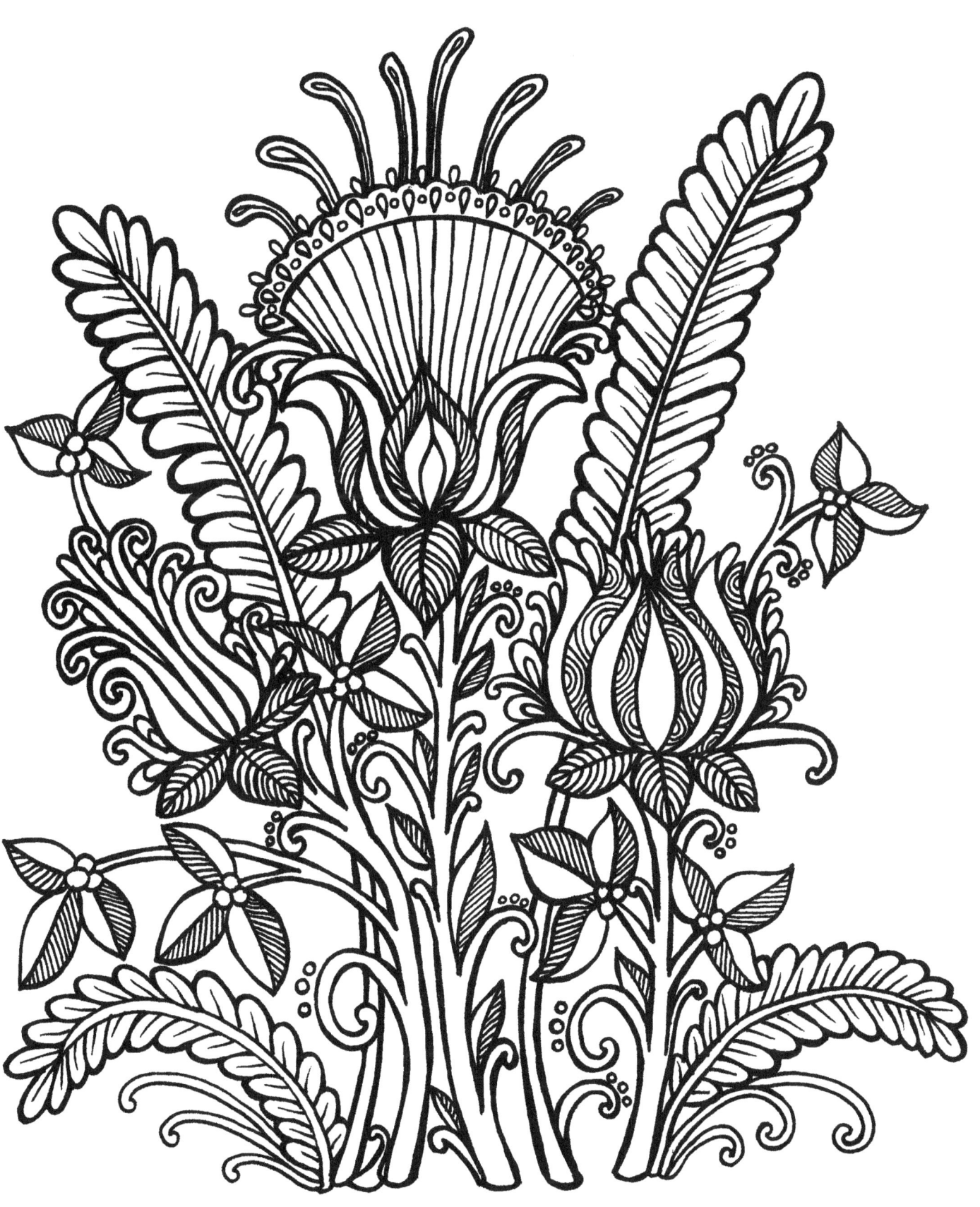

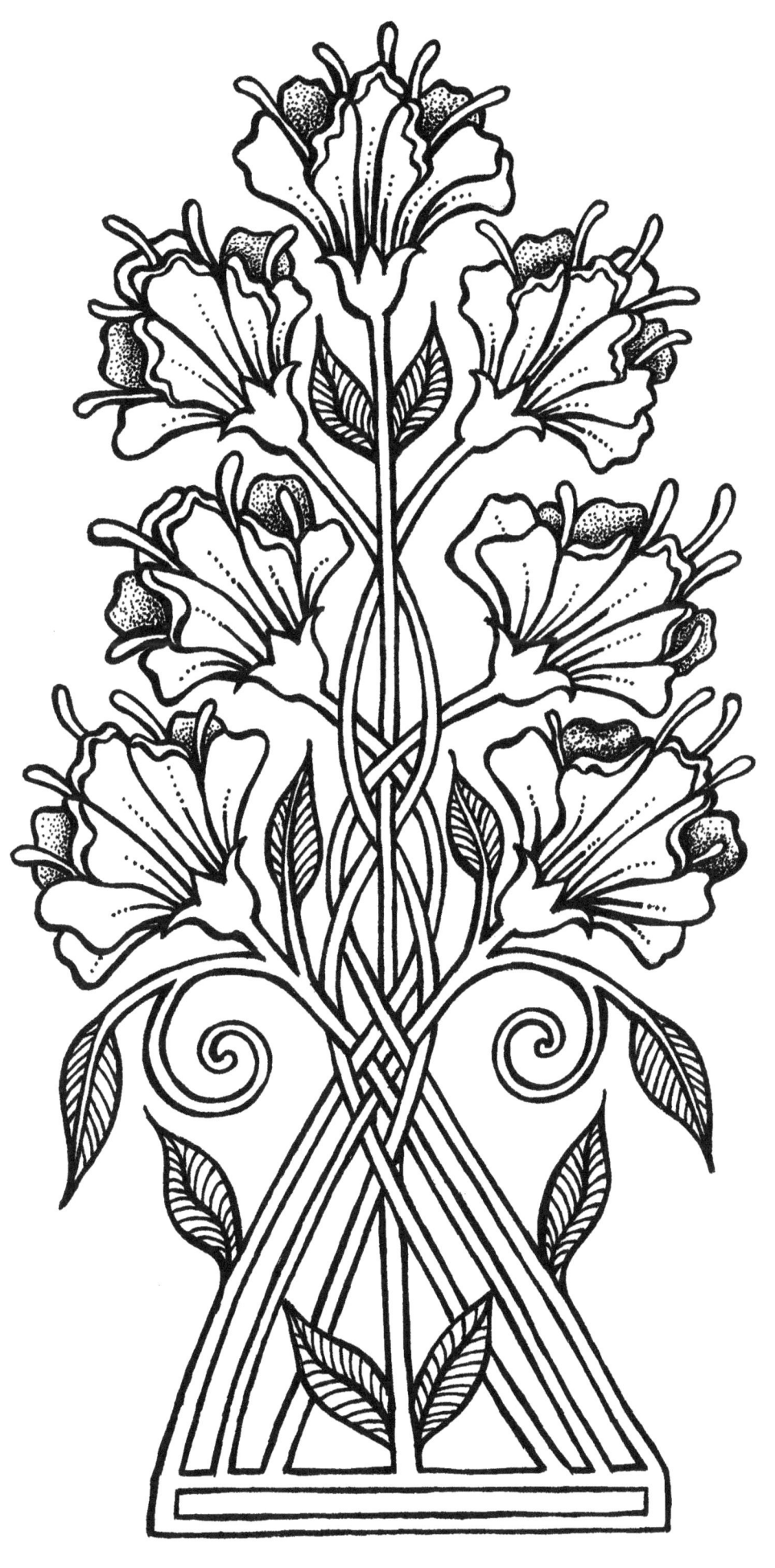

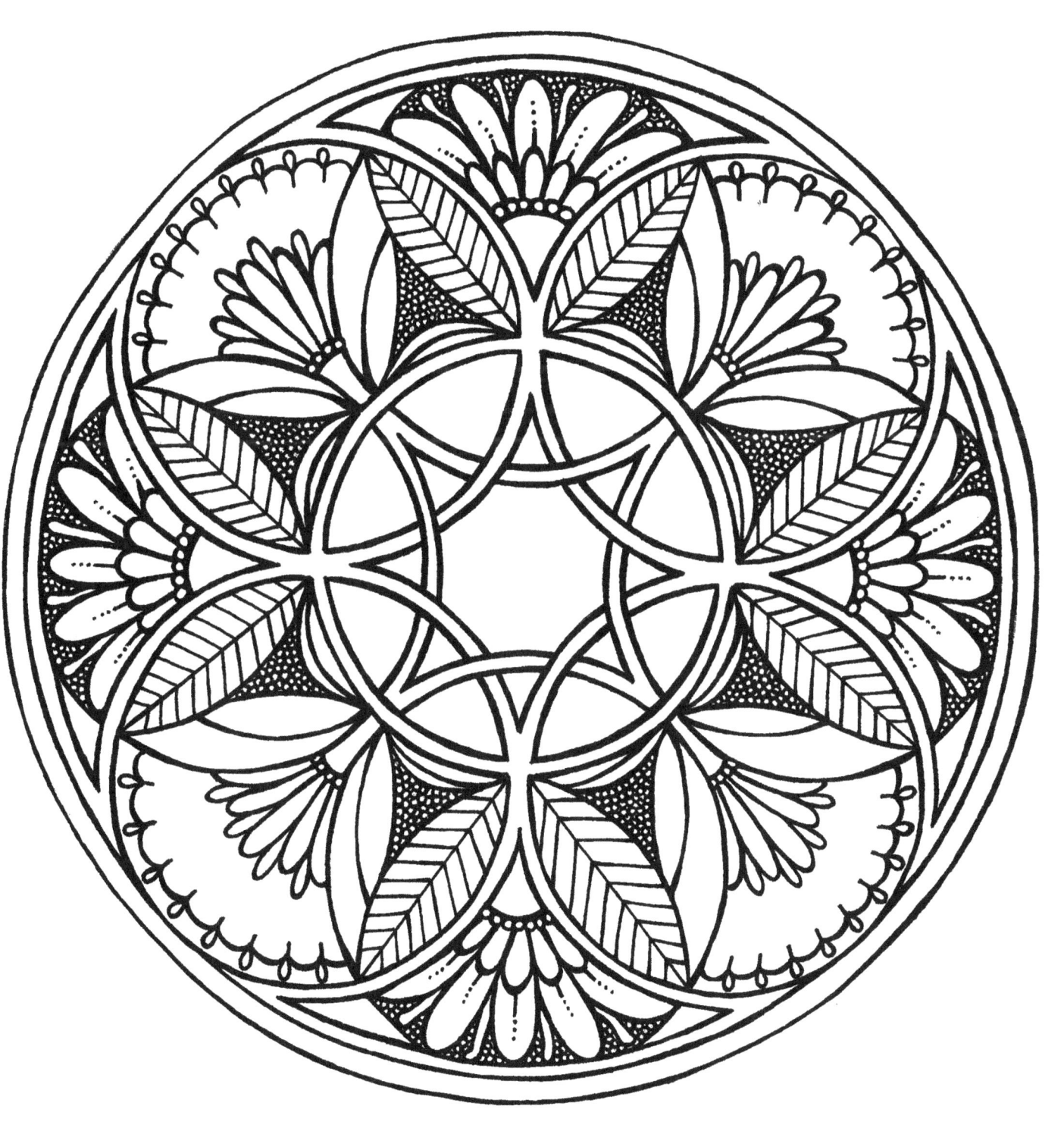

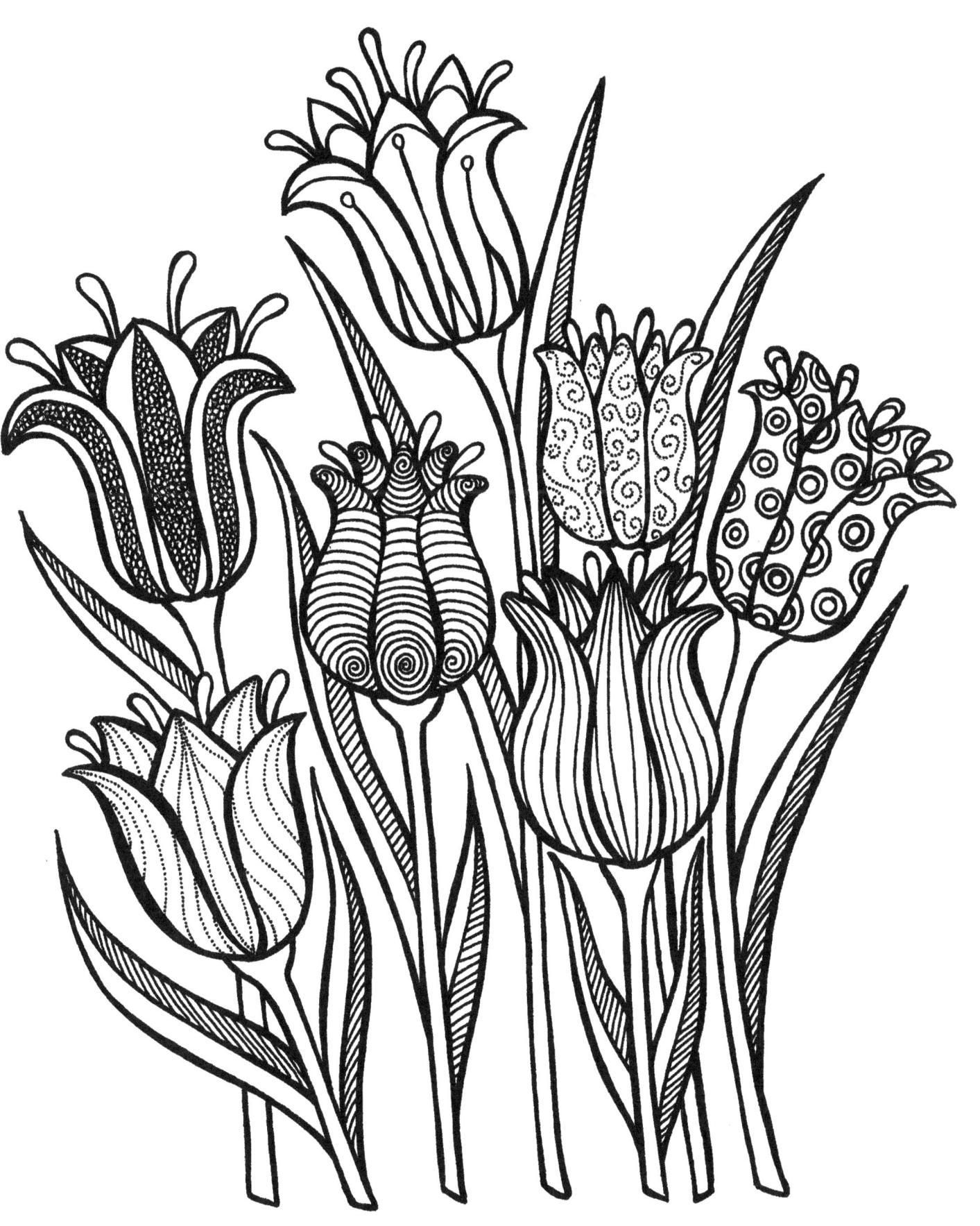

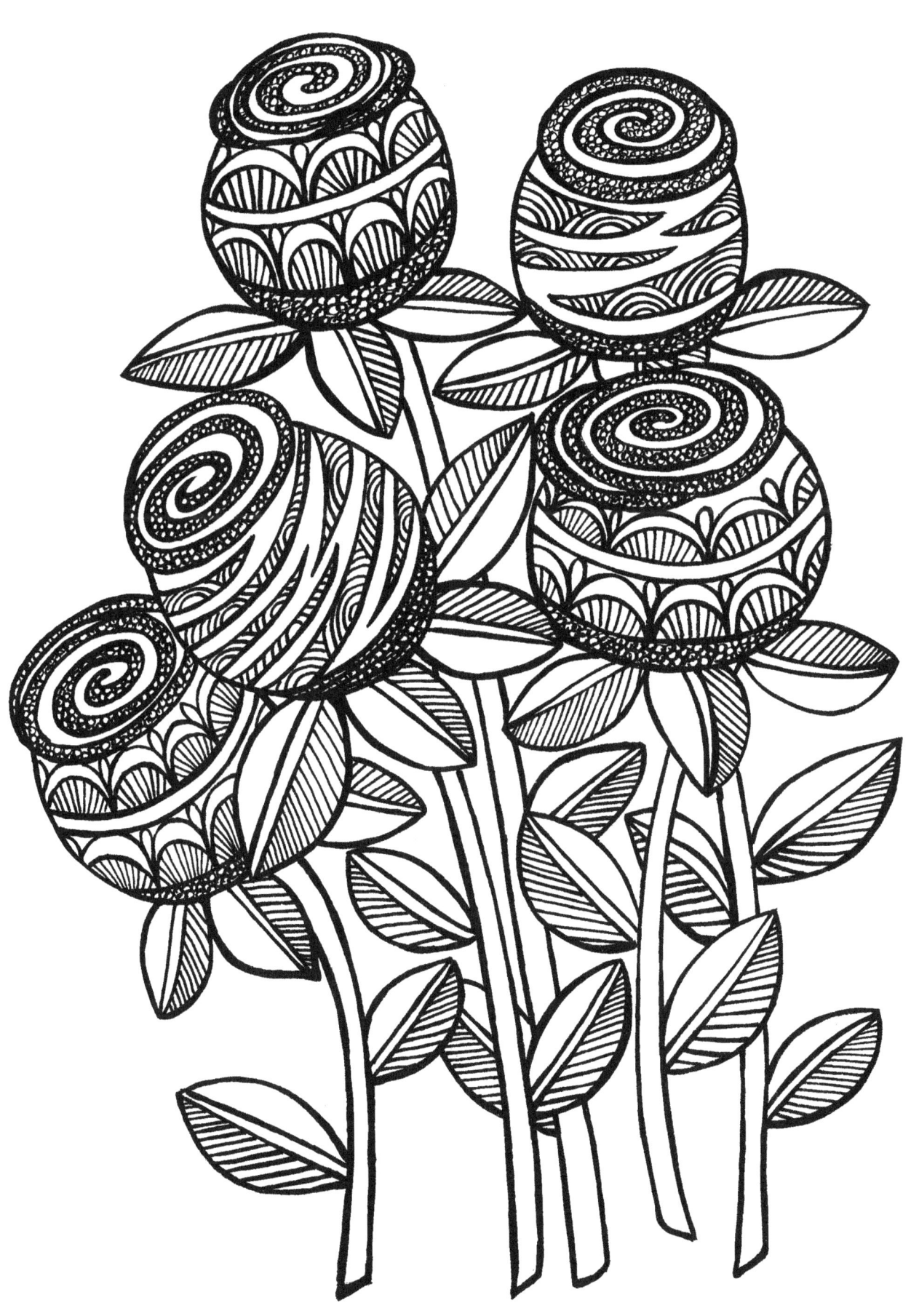

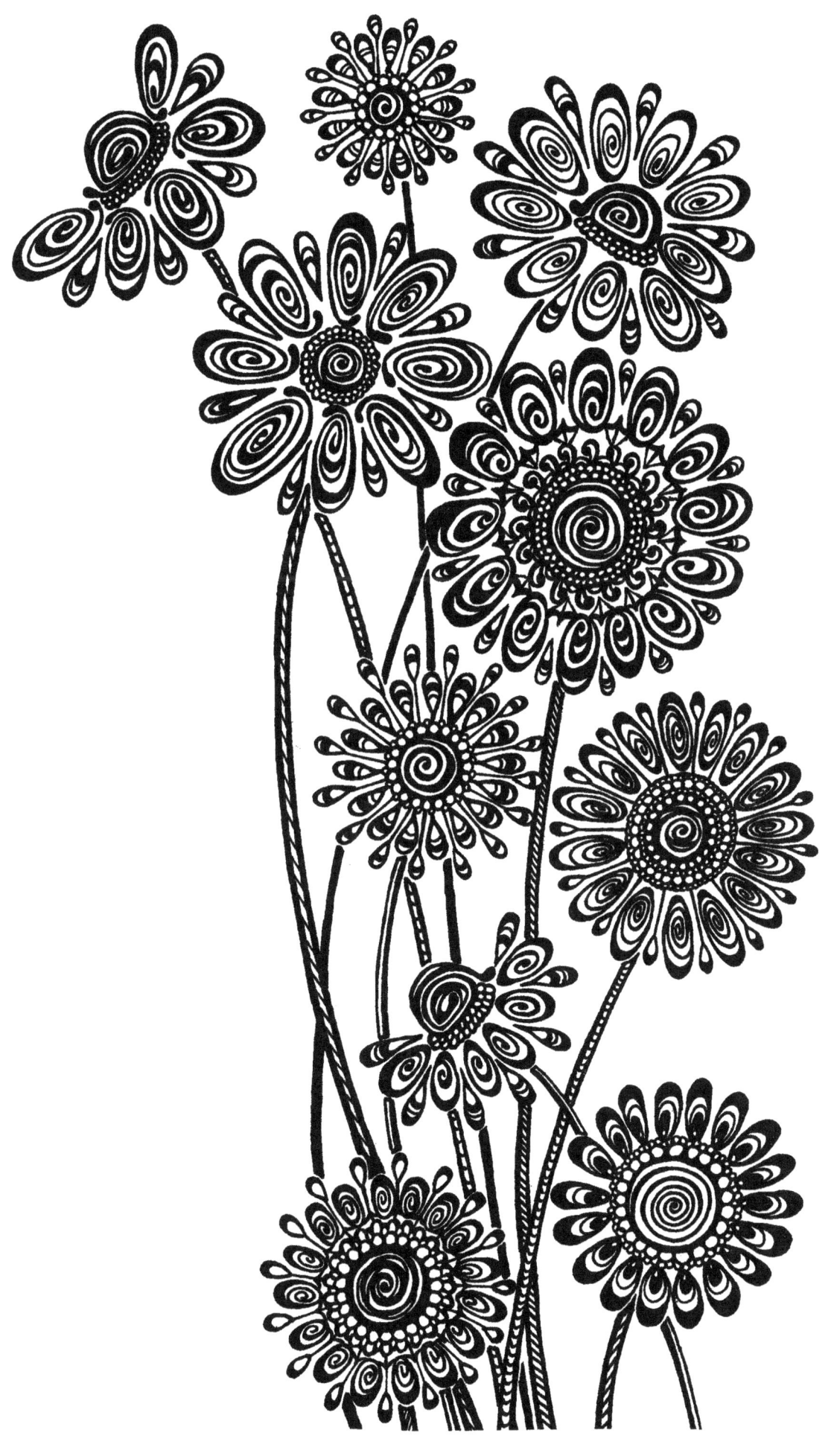

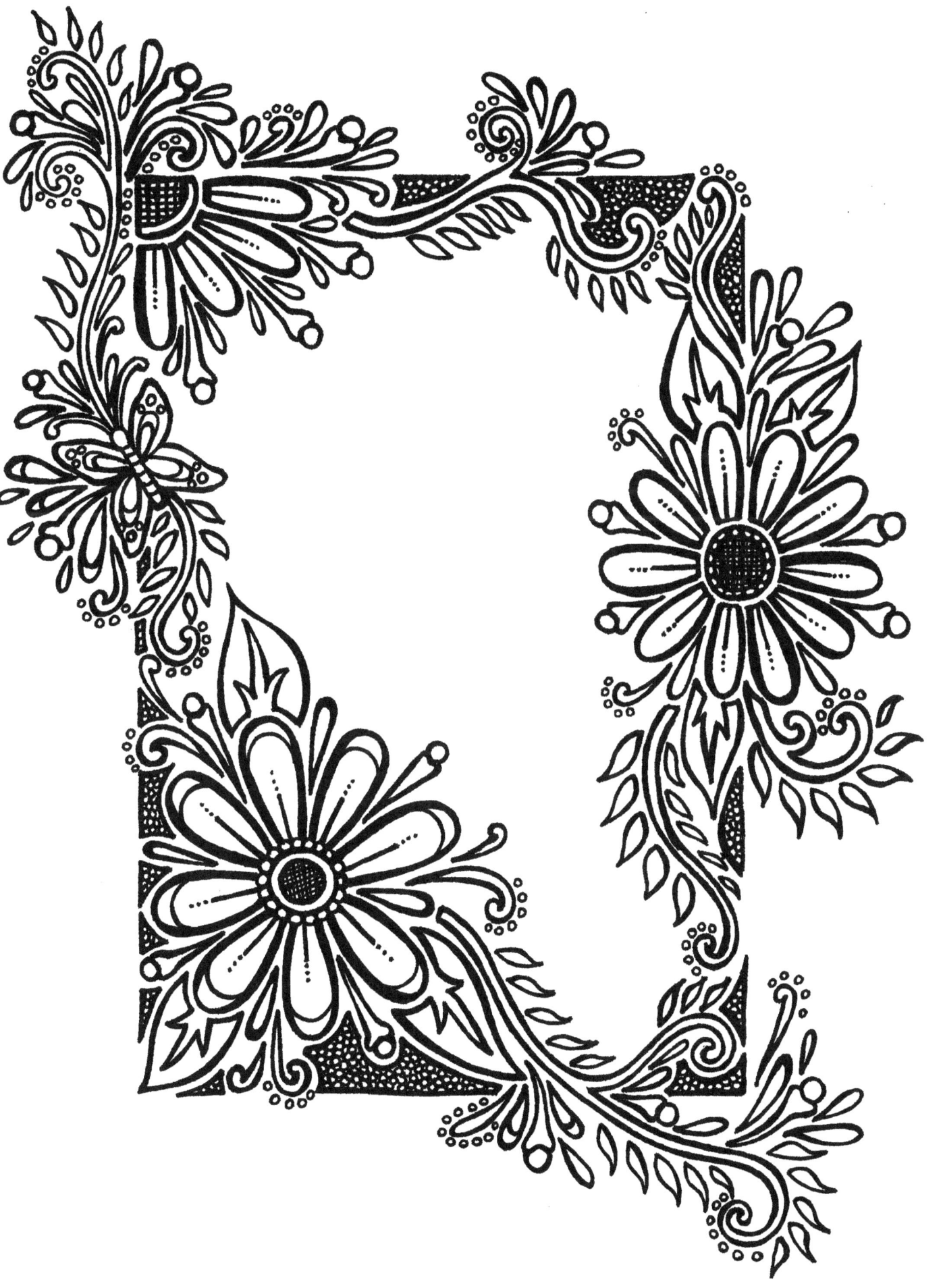

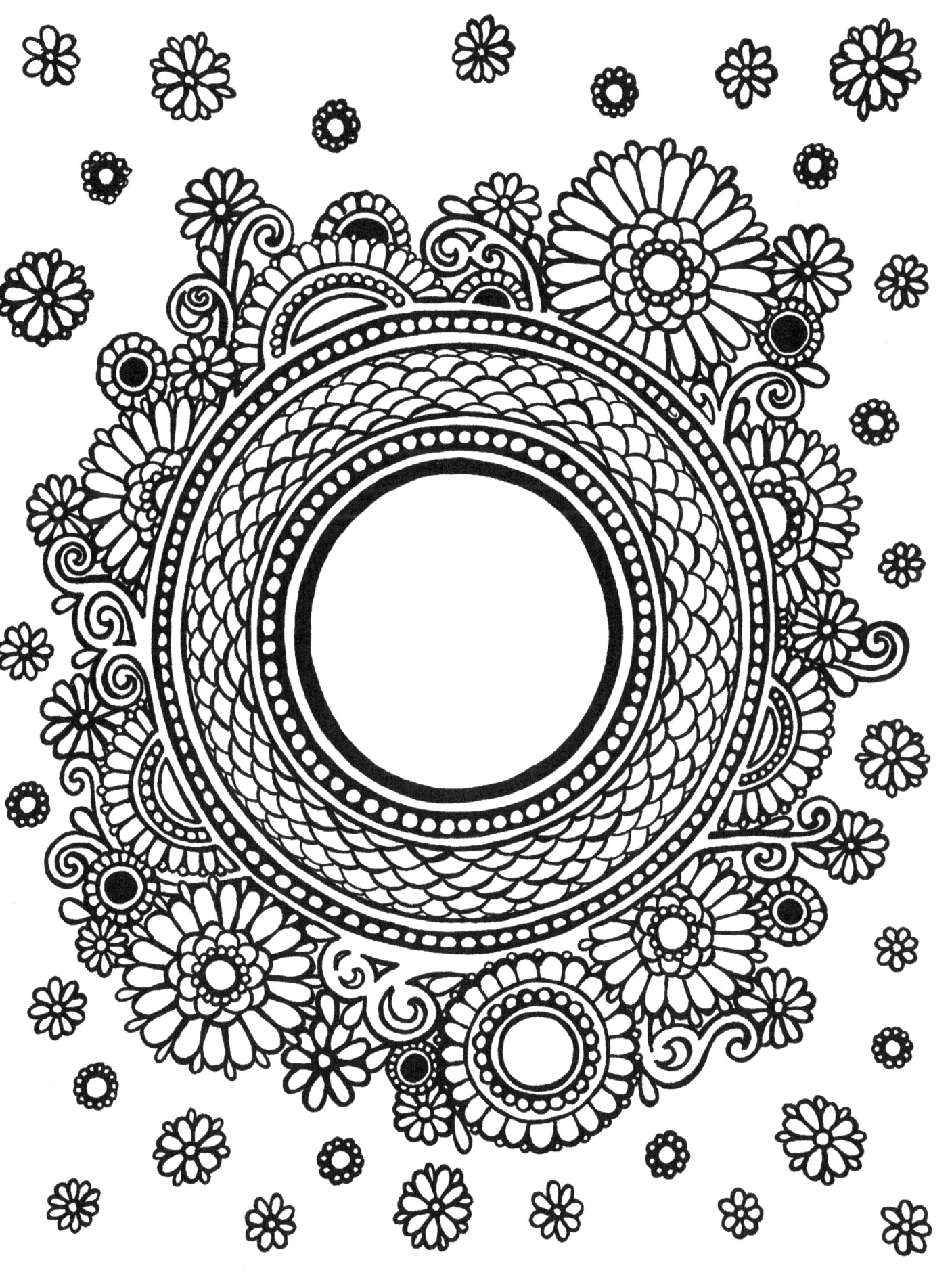

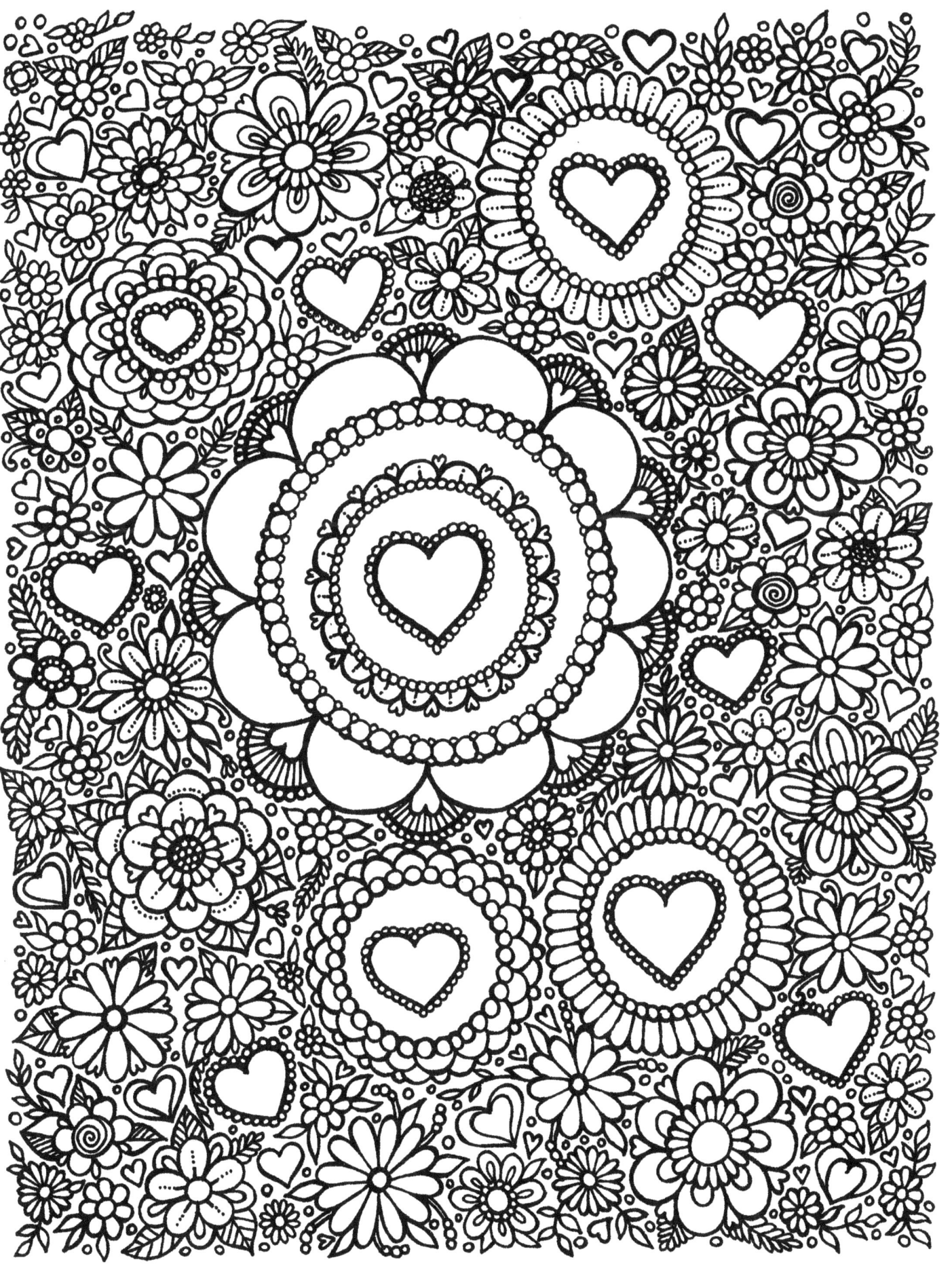

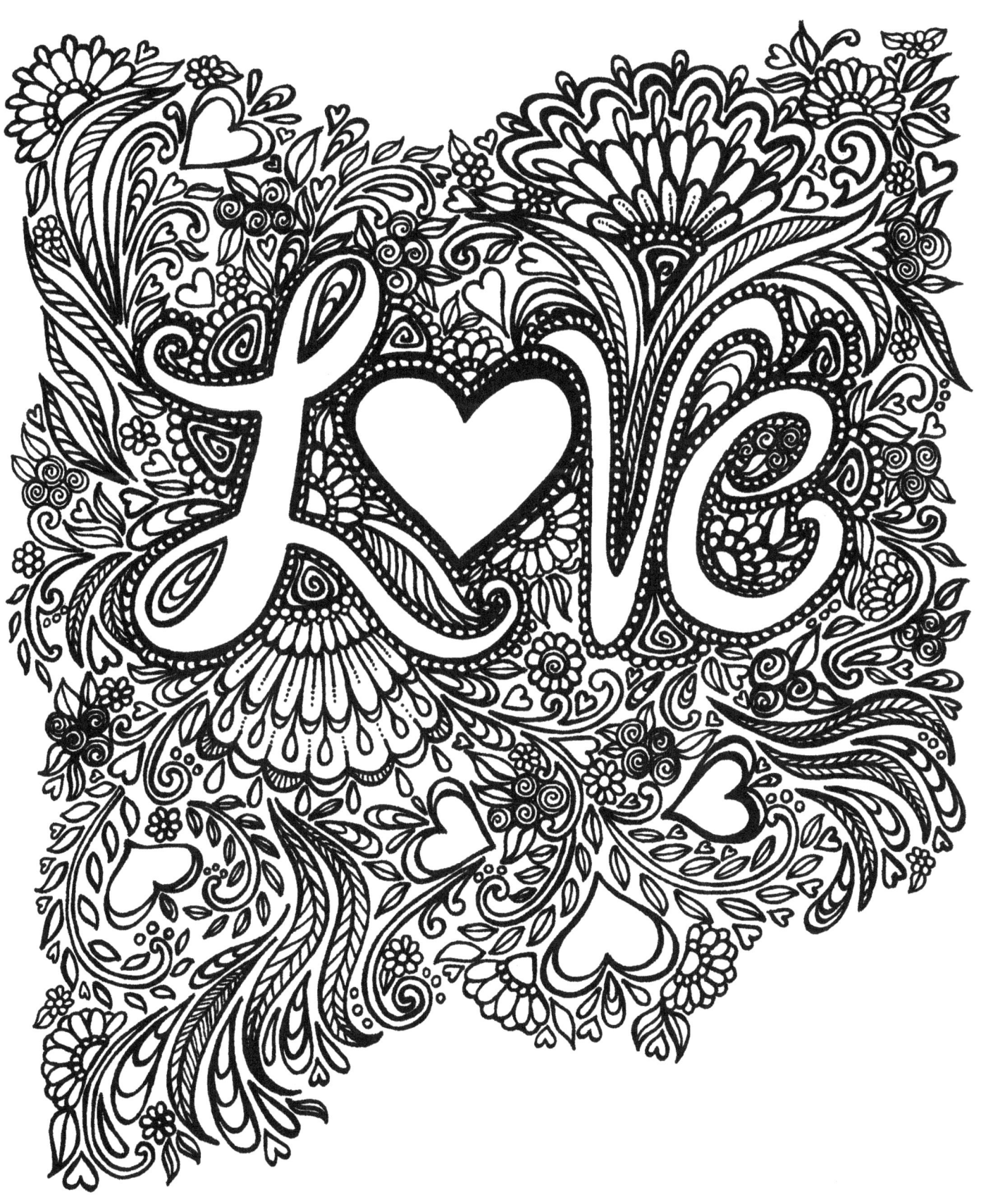

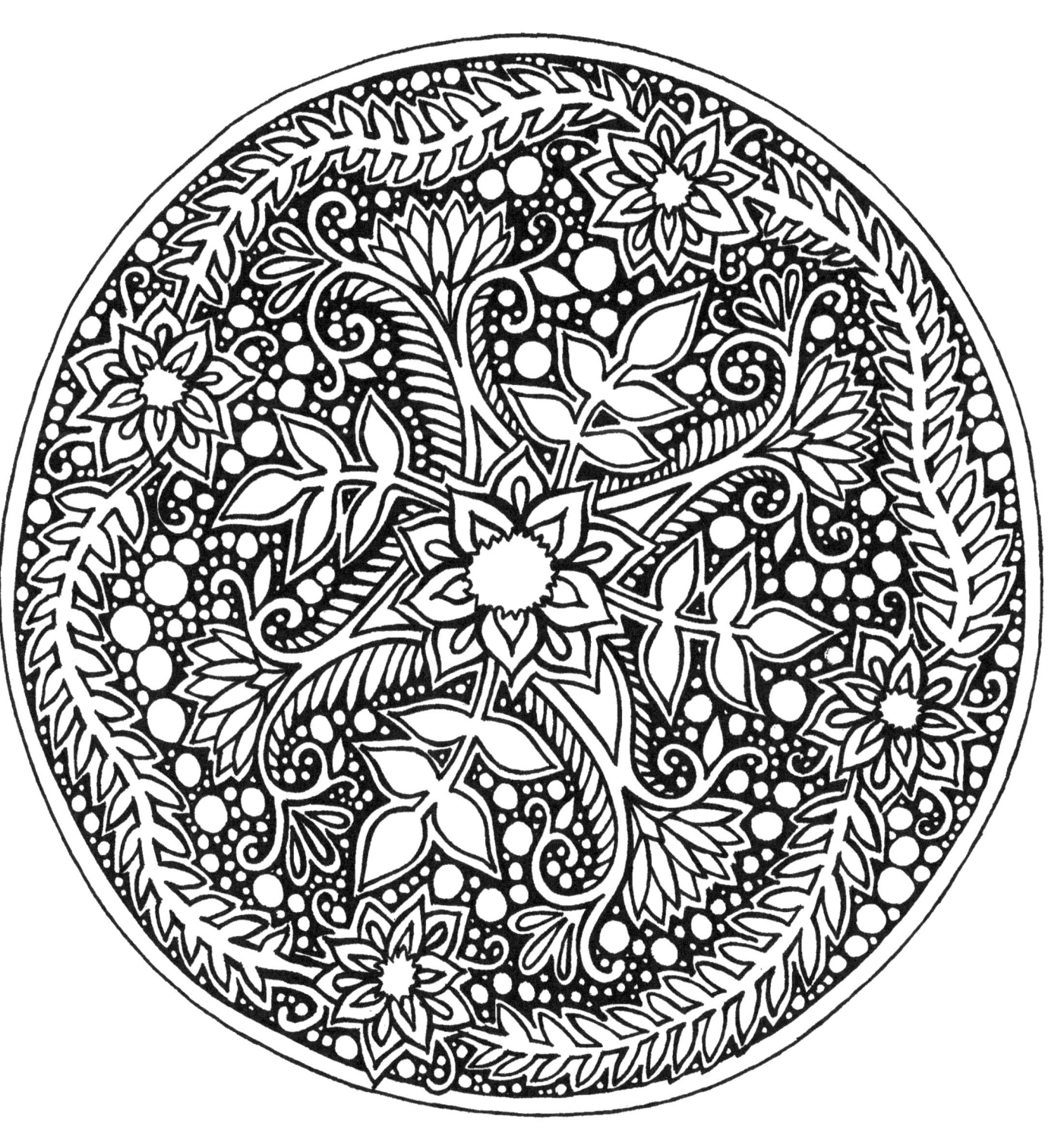

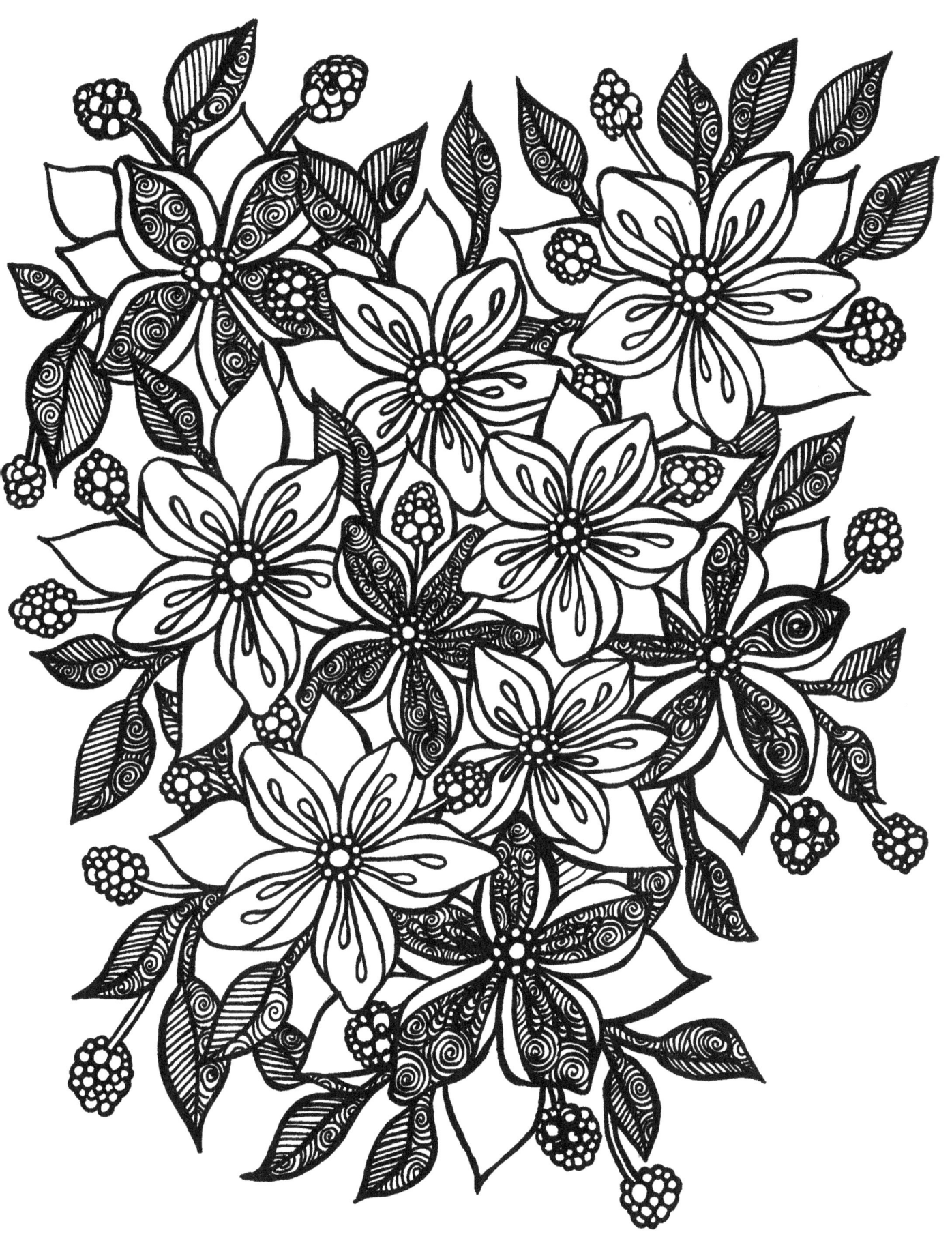

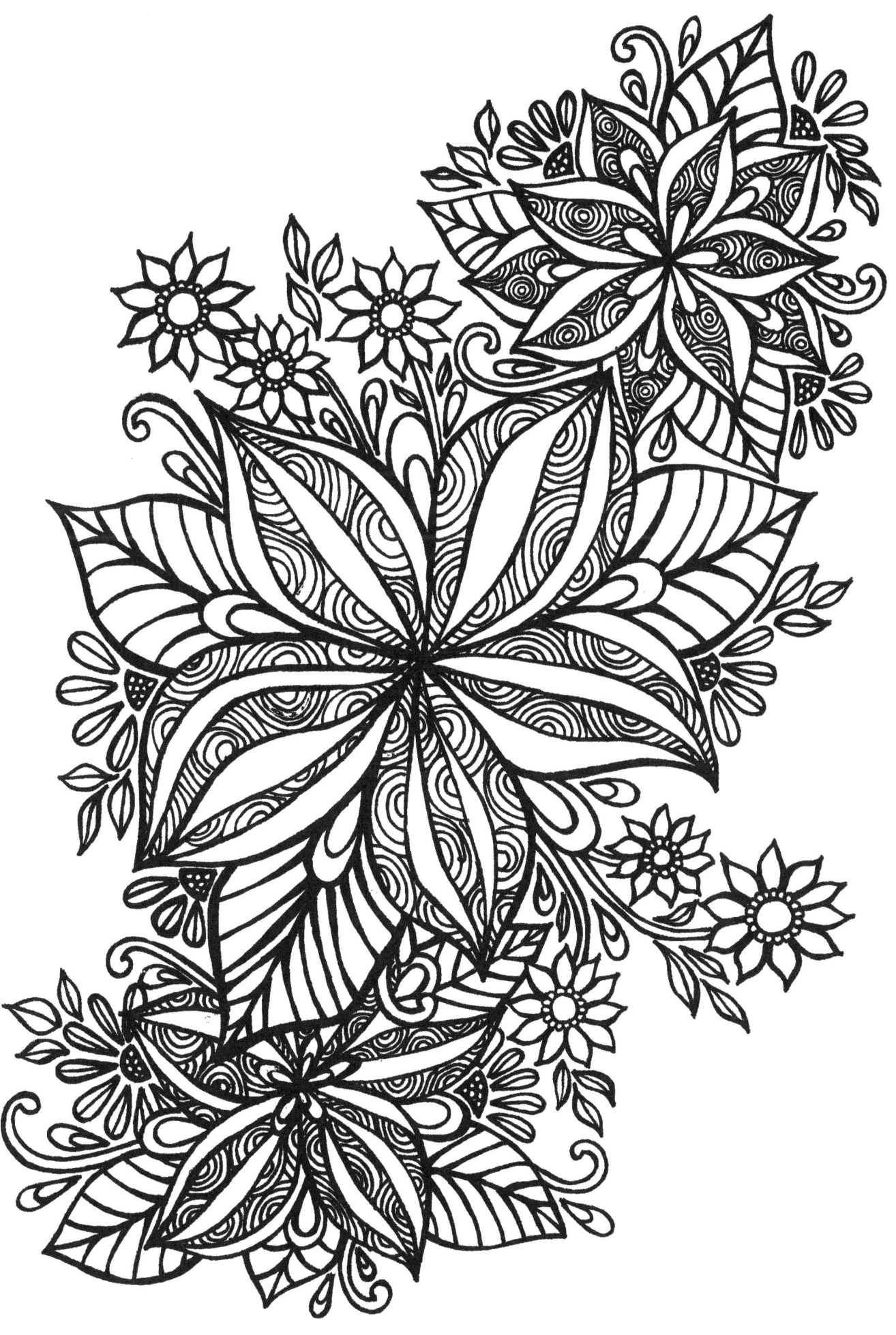

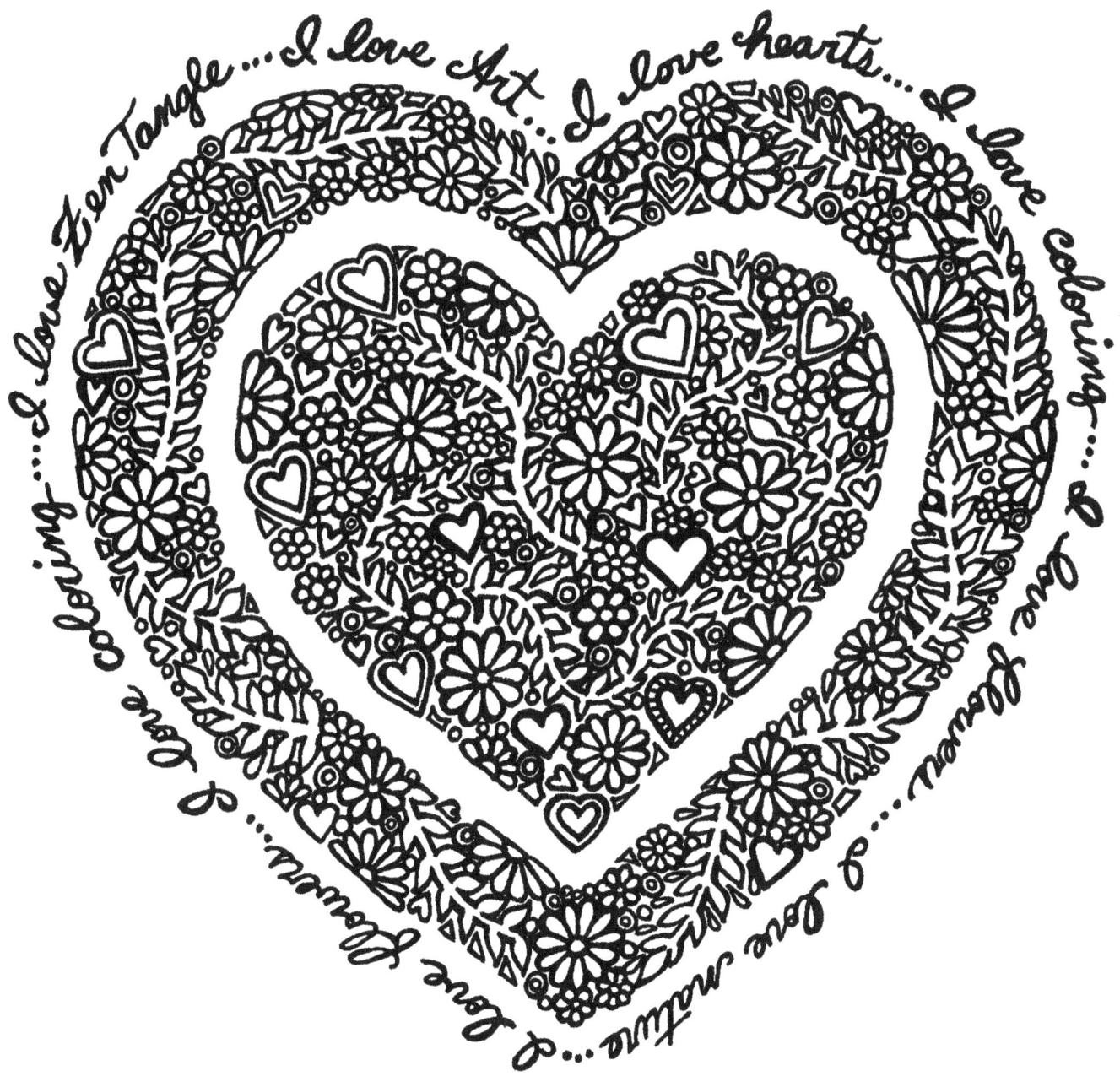

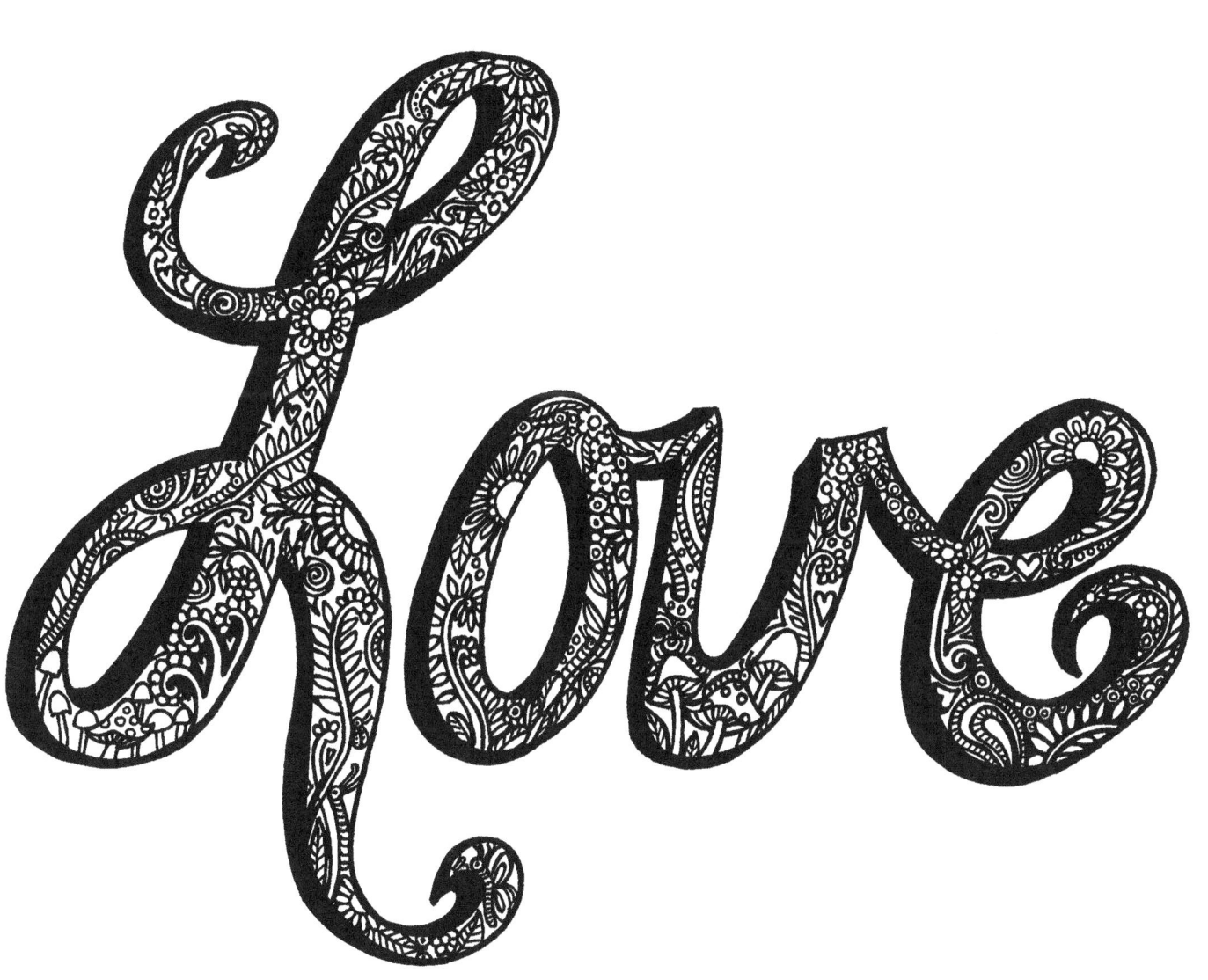

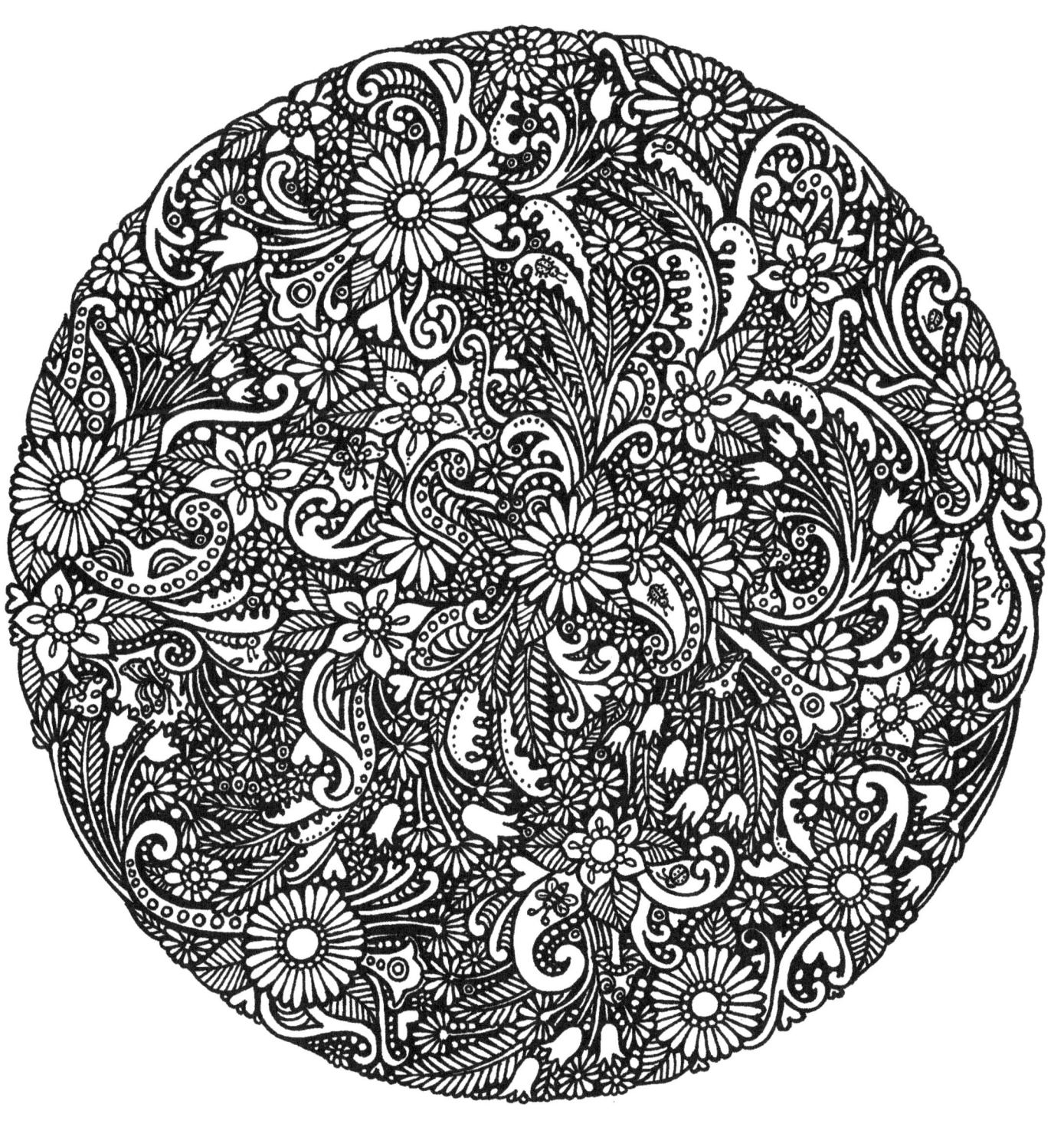

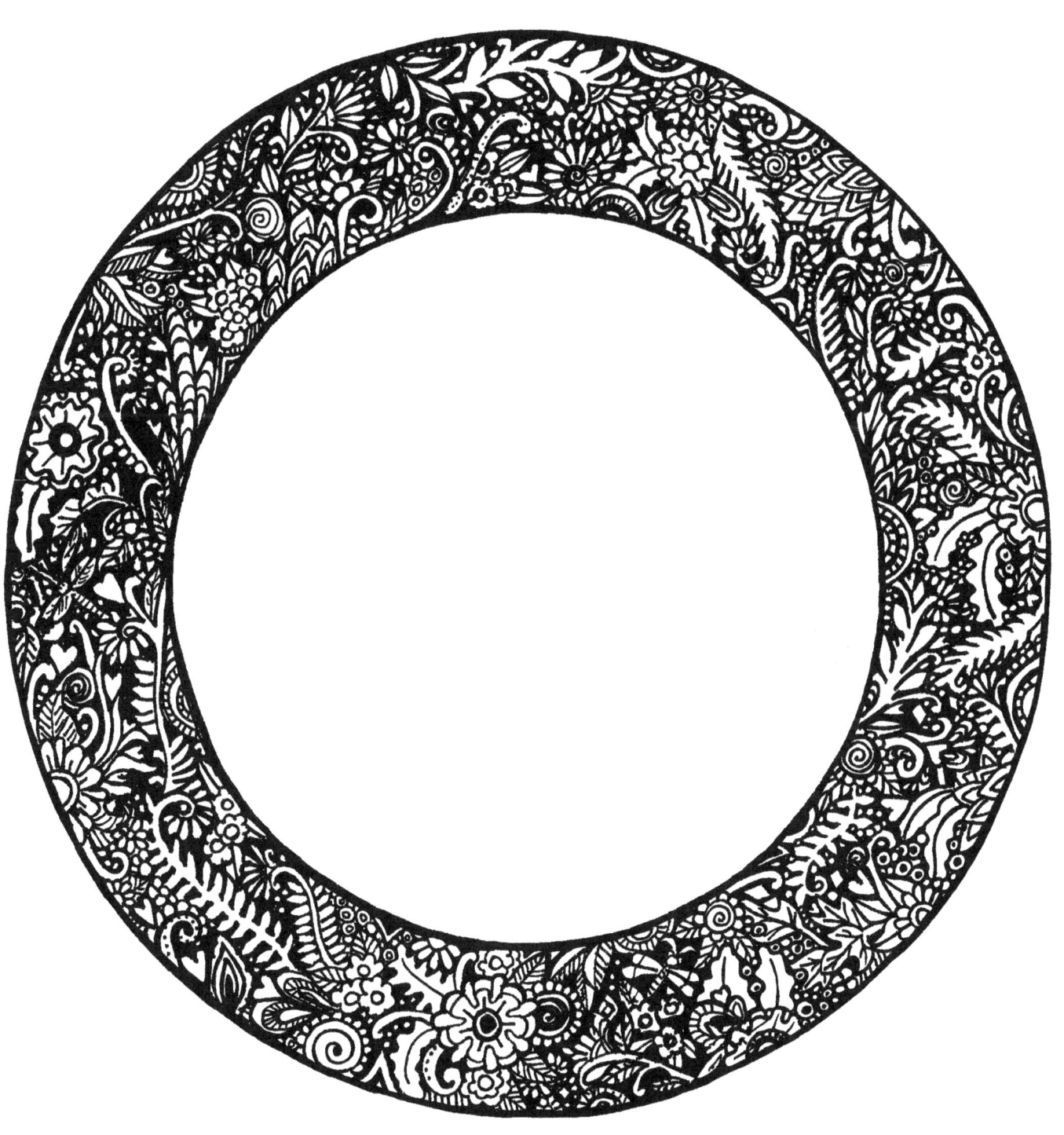

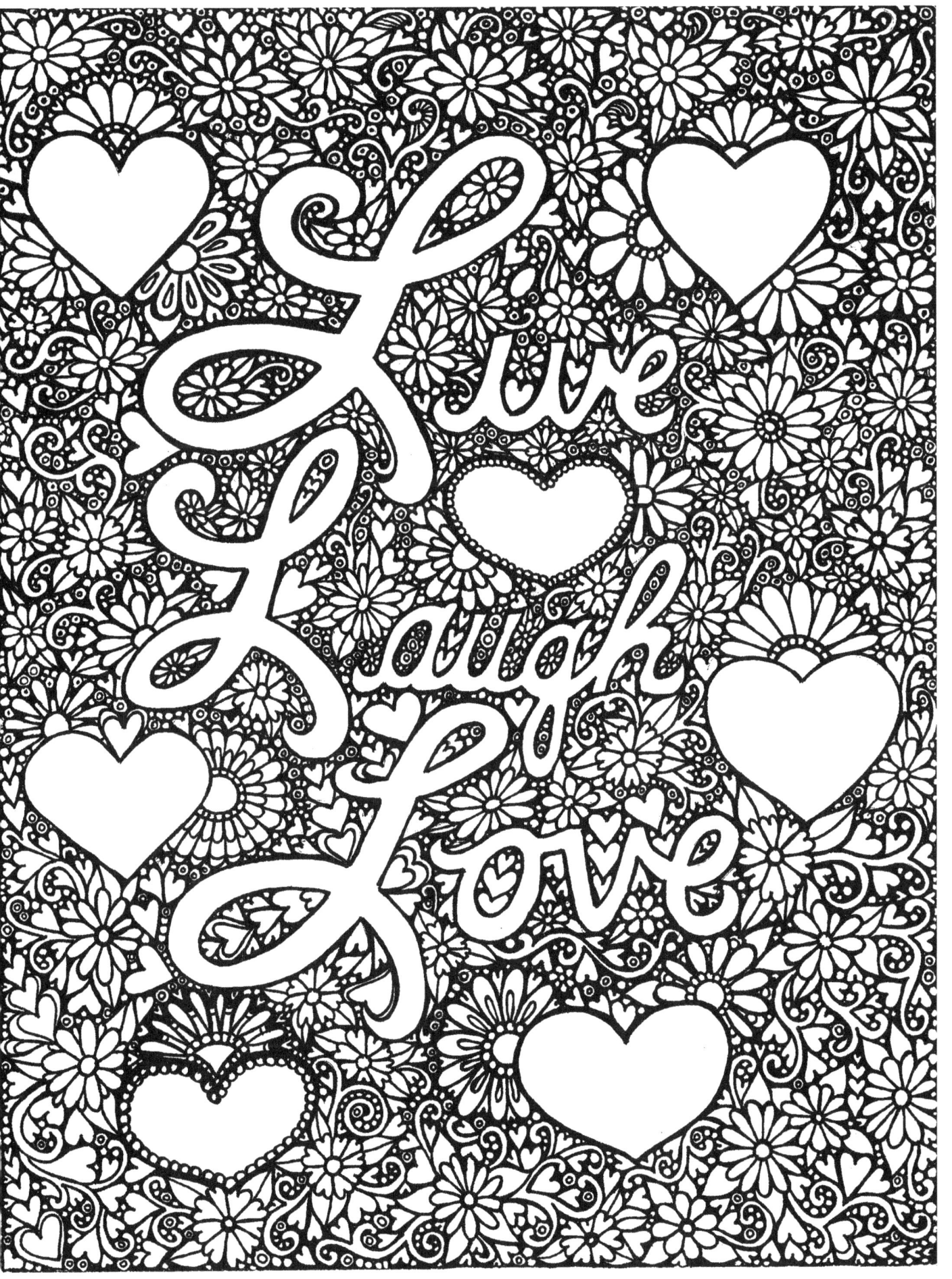

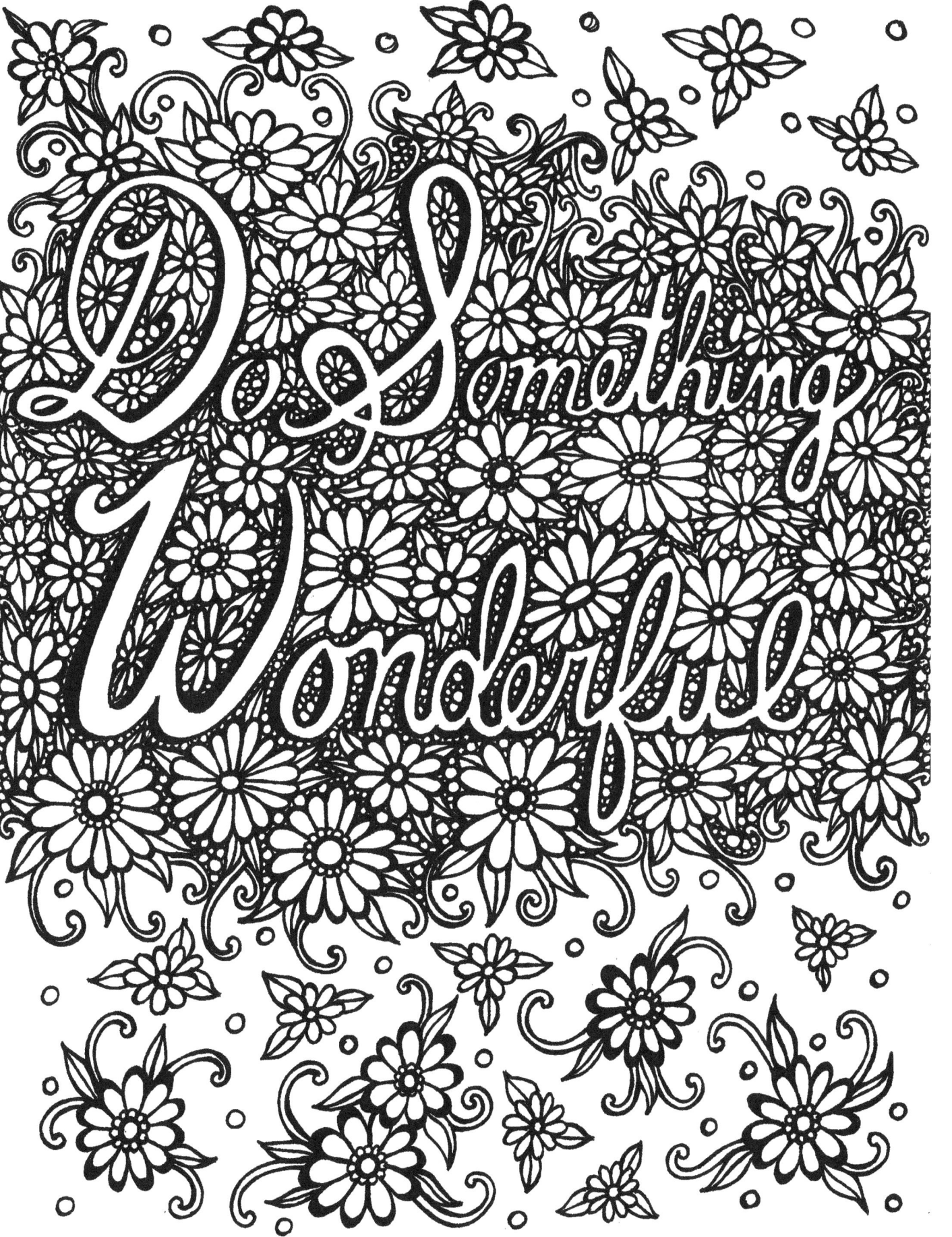

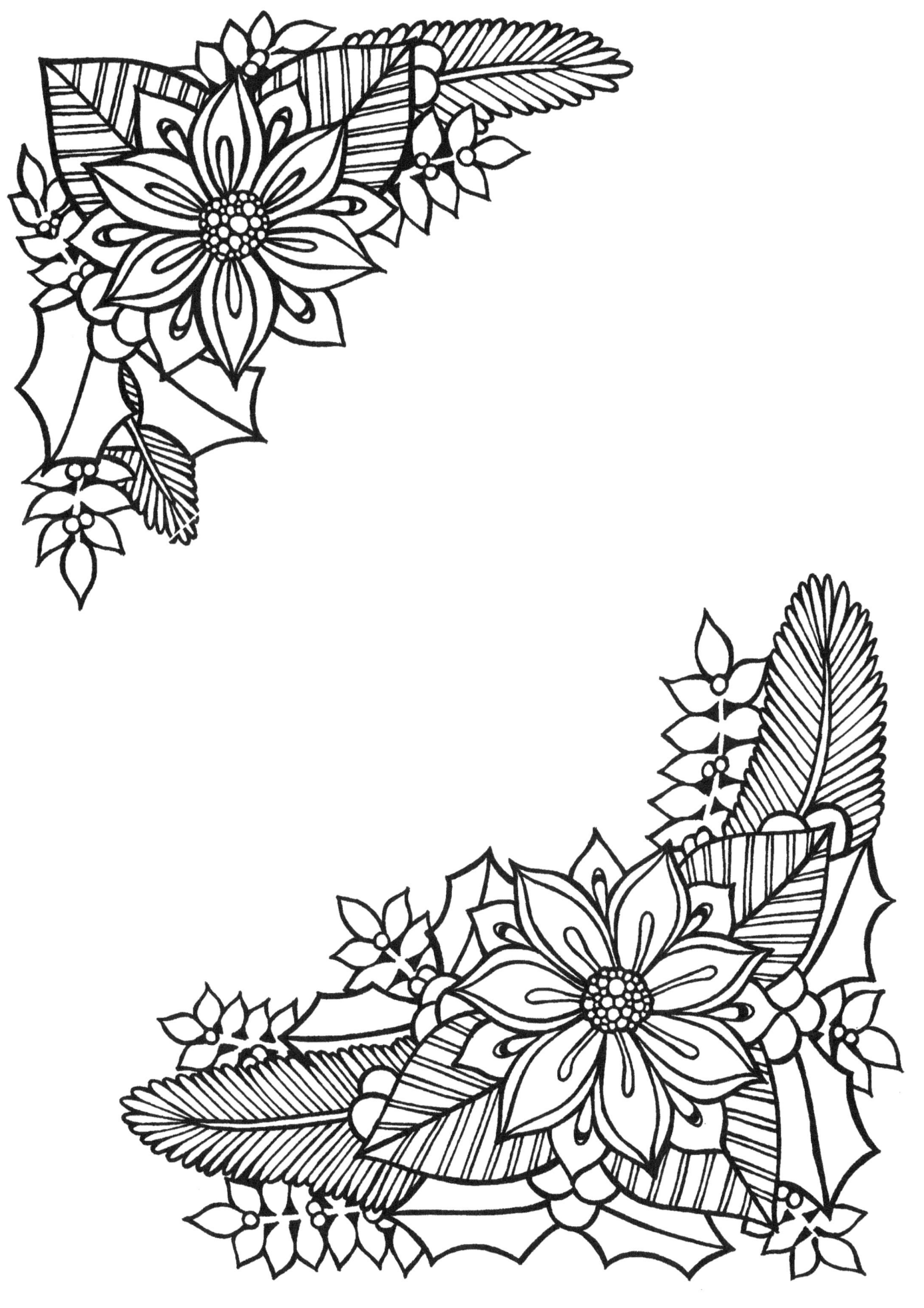

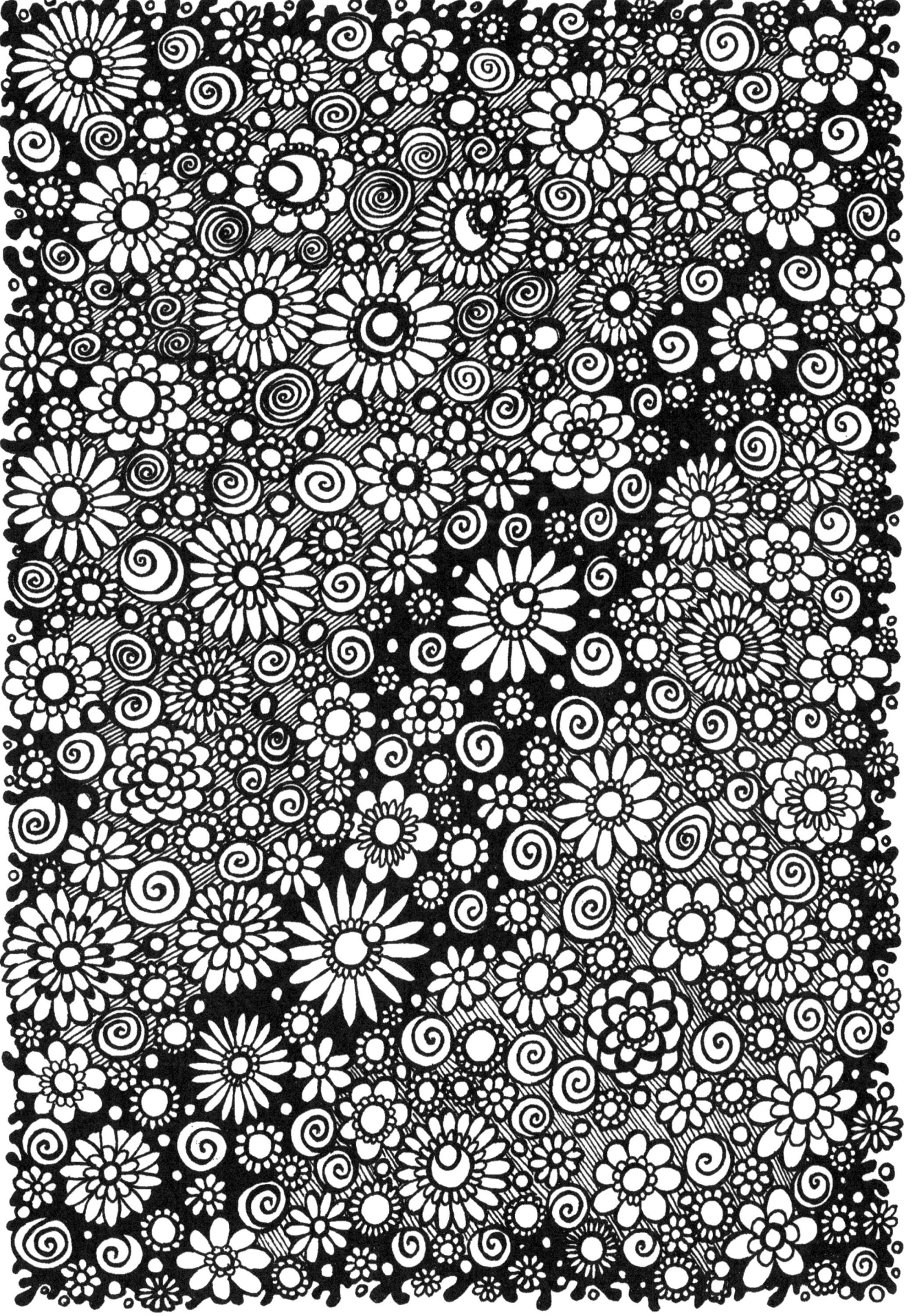

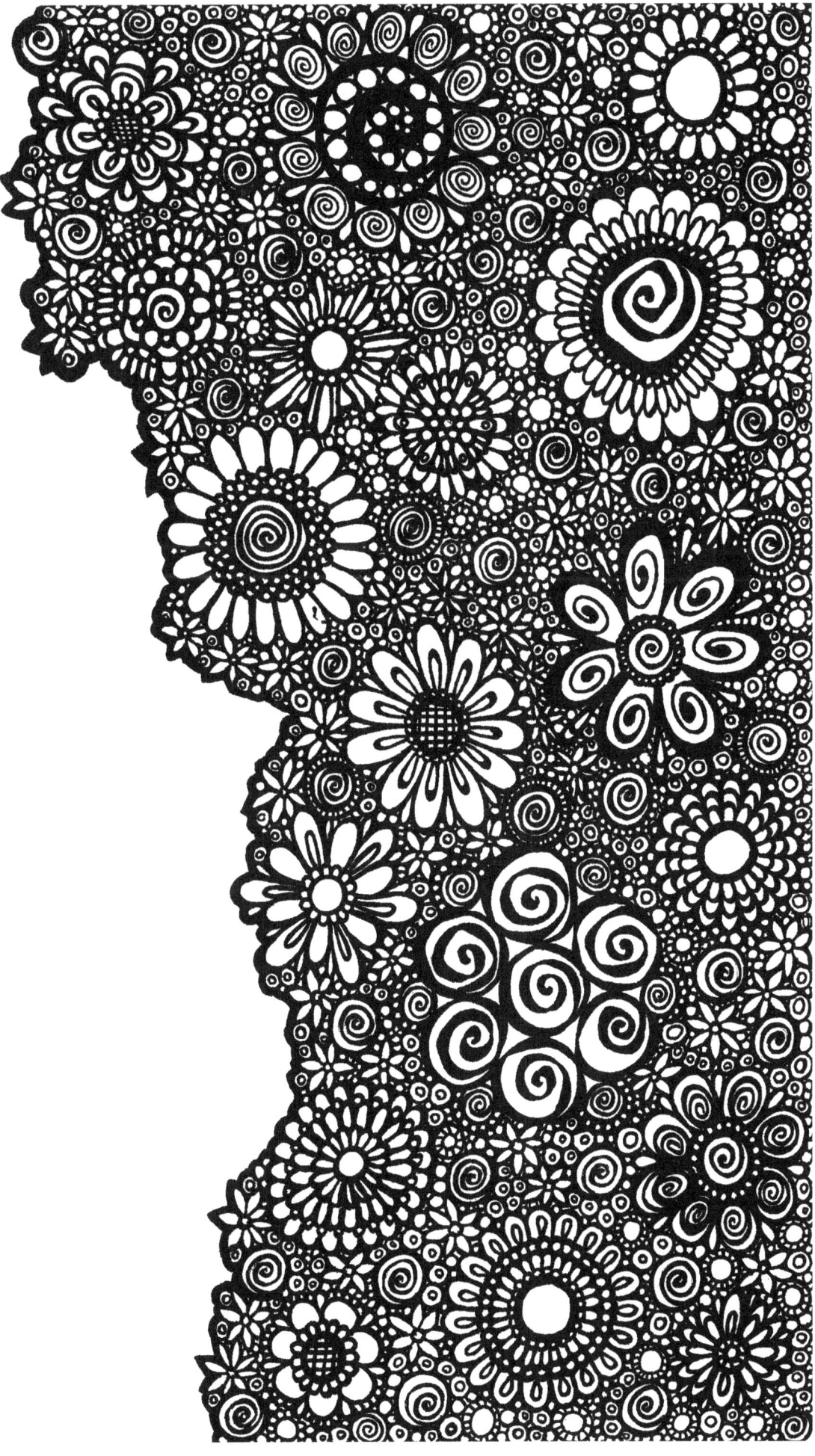

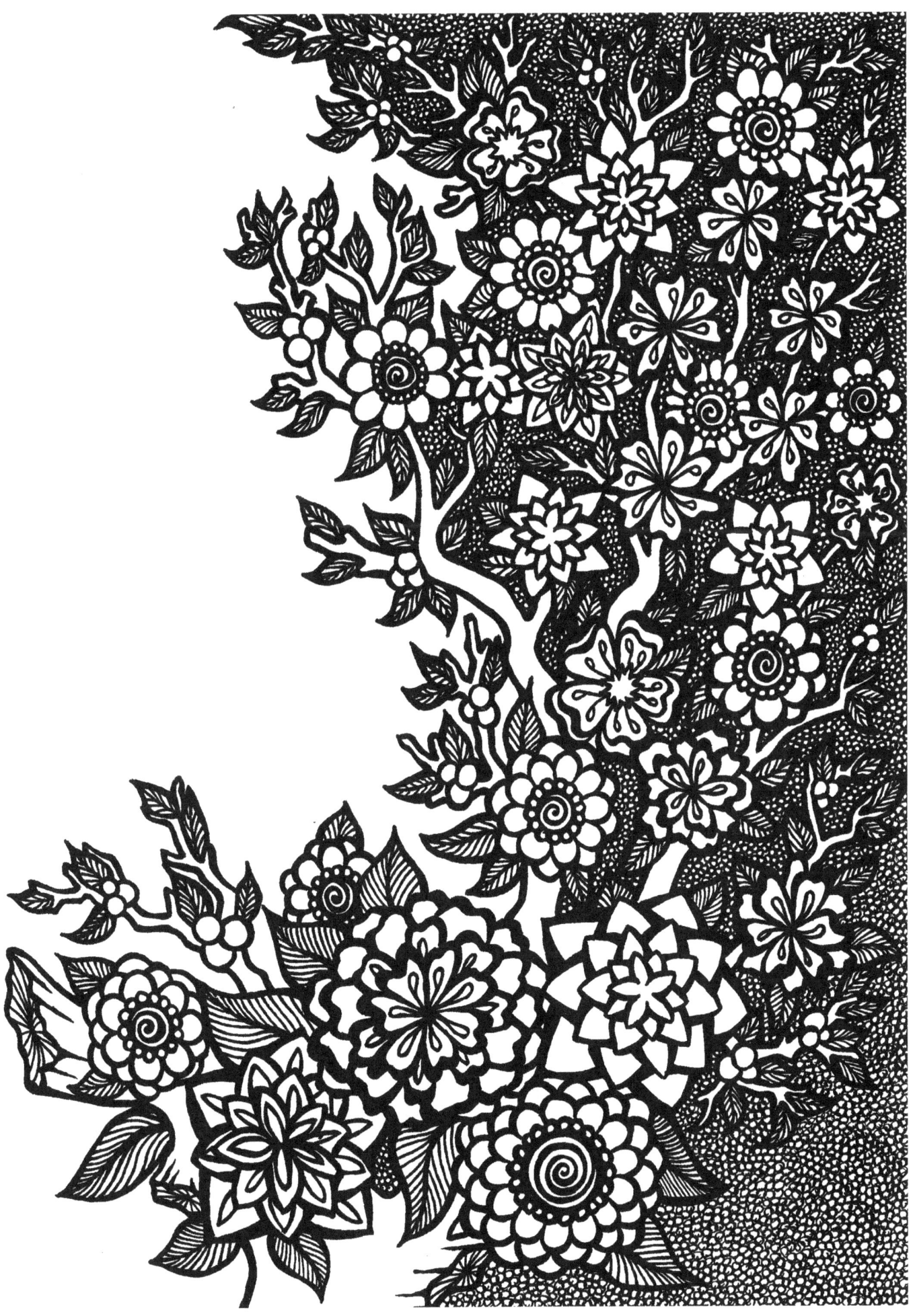

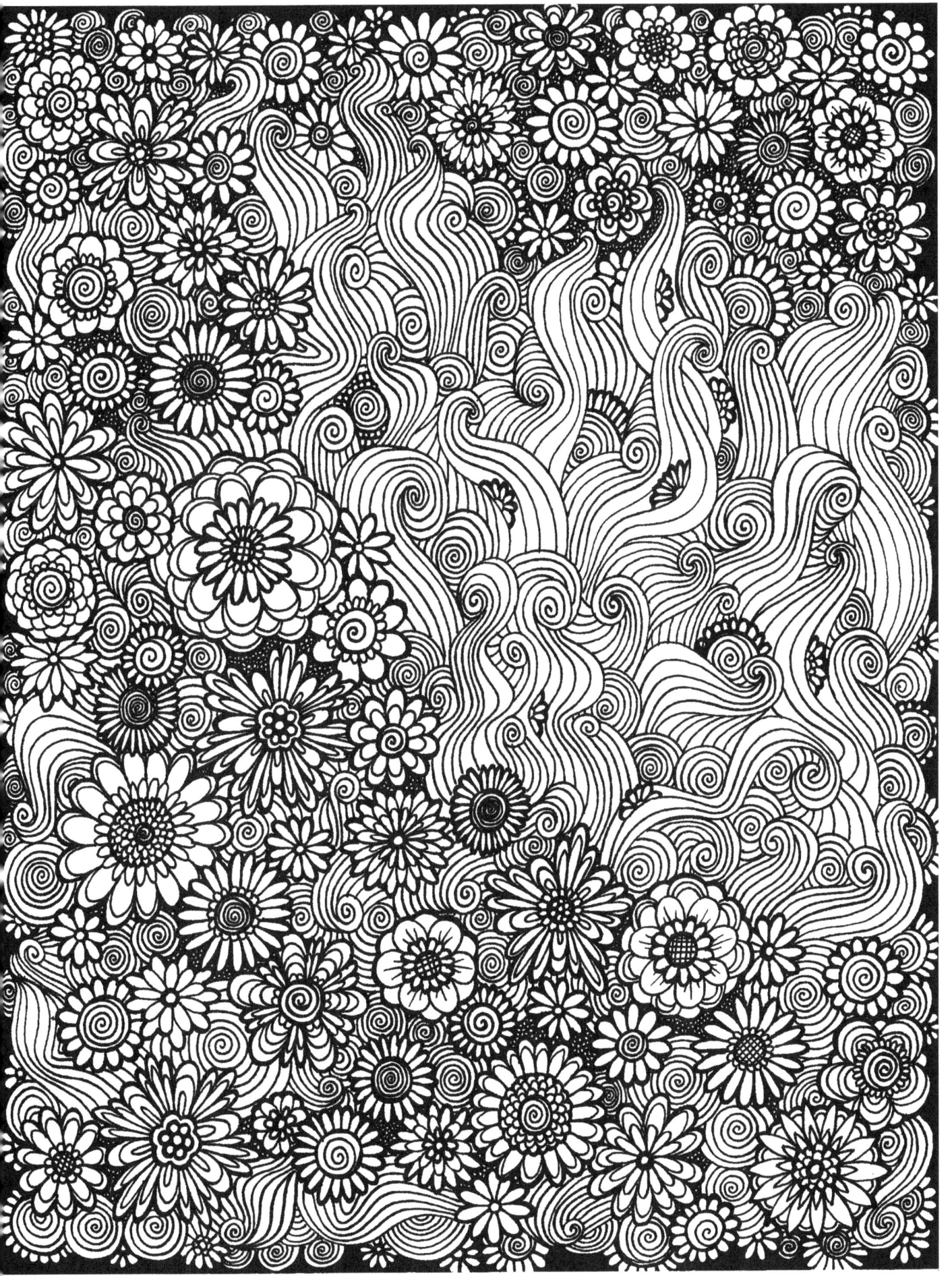

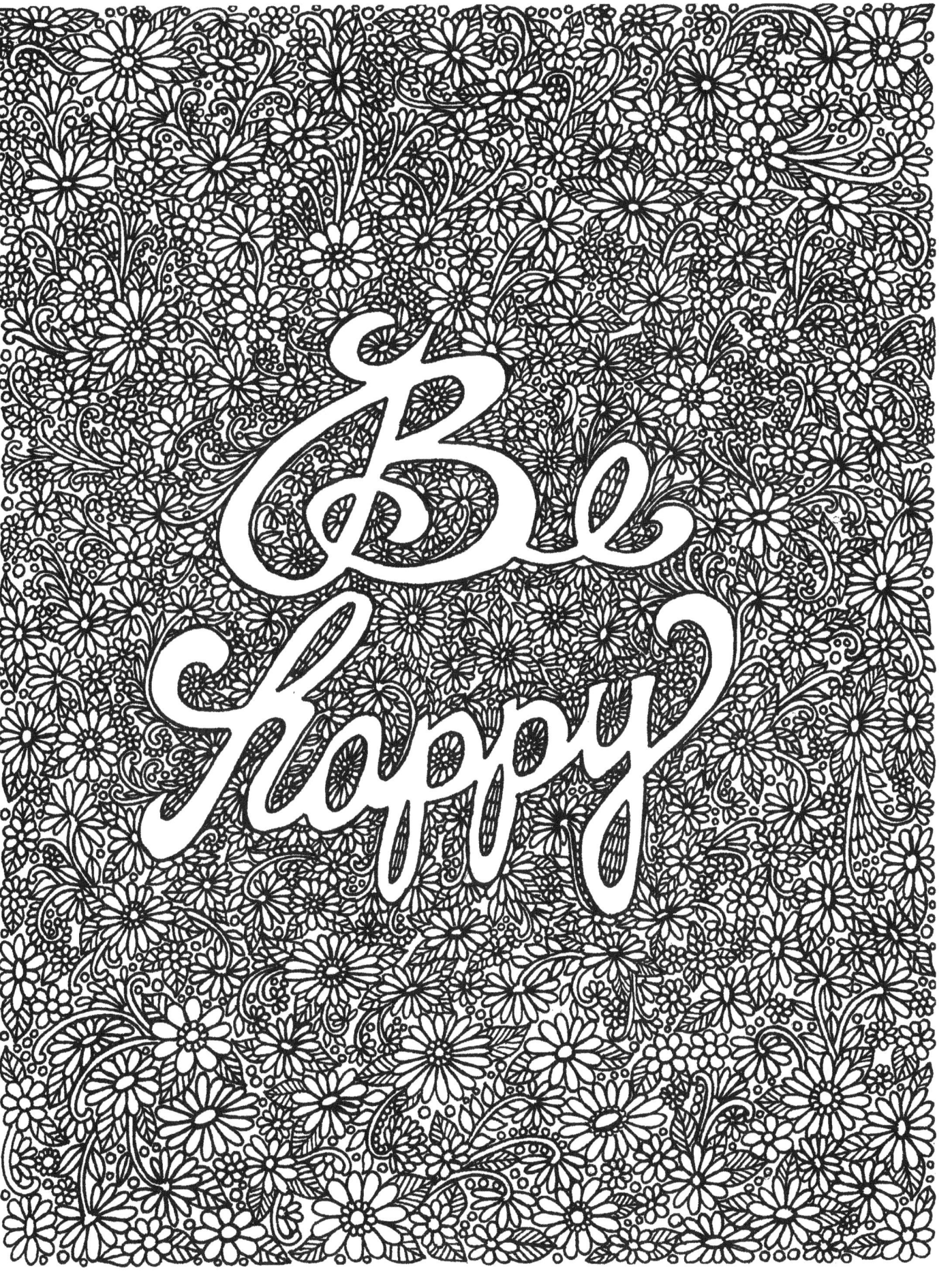

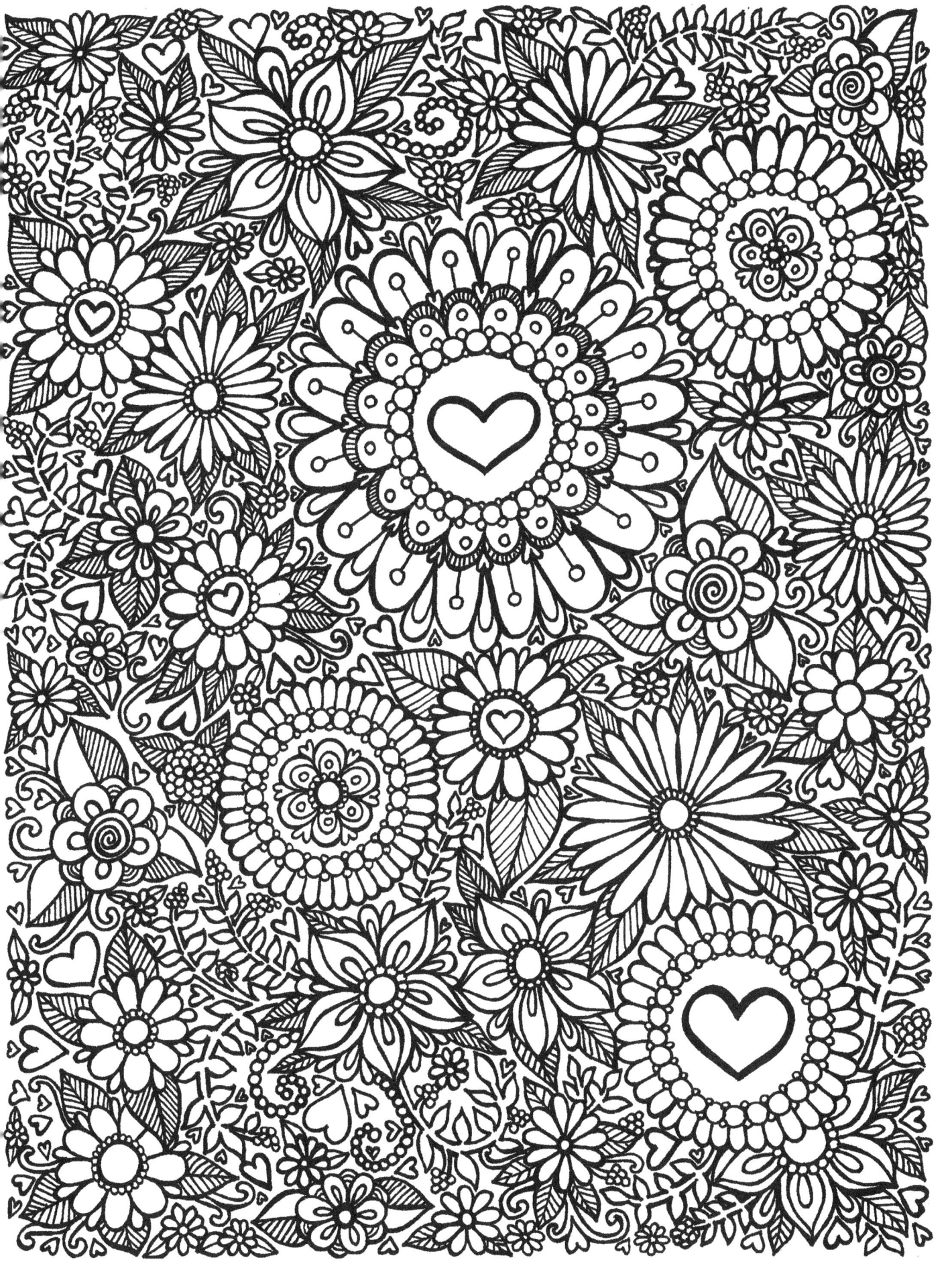

Color your own bookmarks.

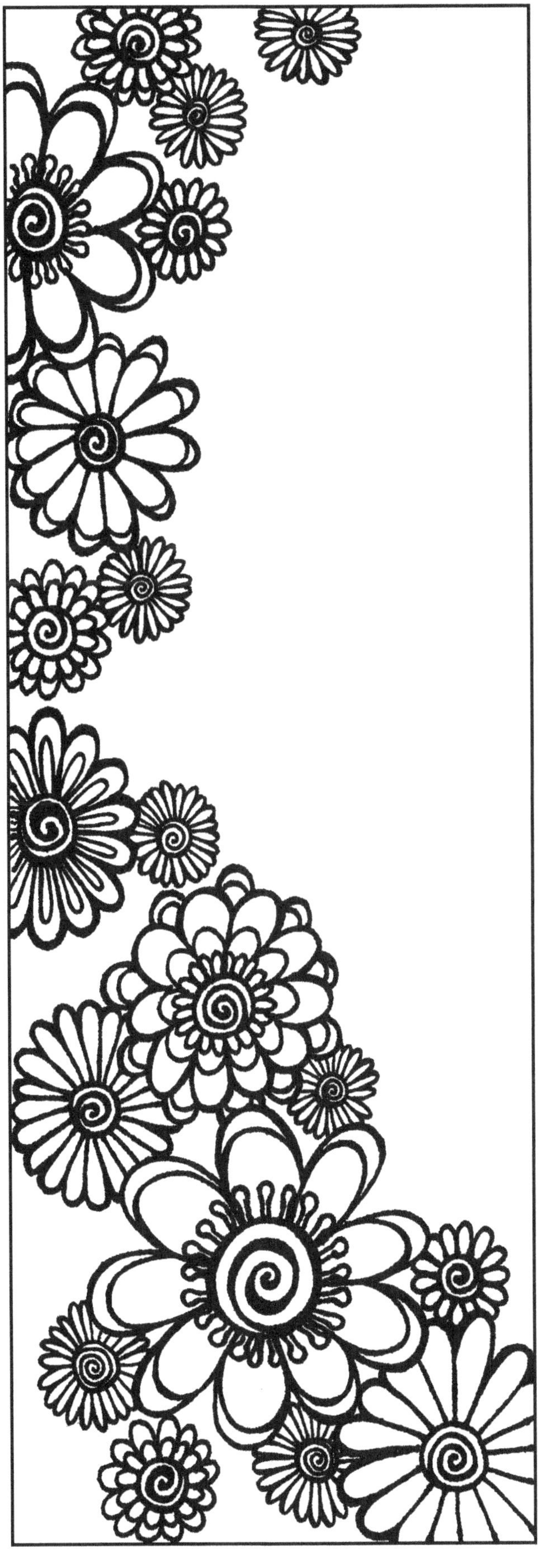

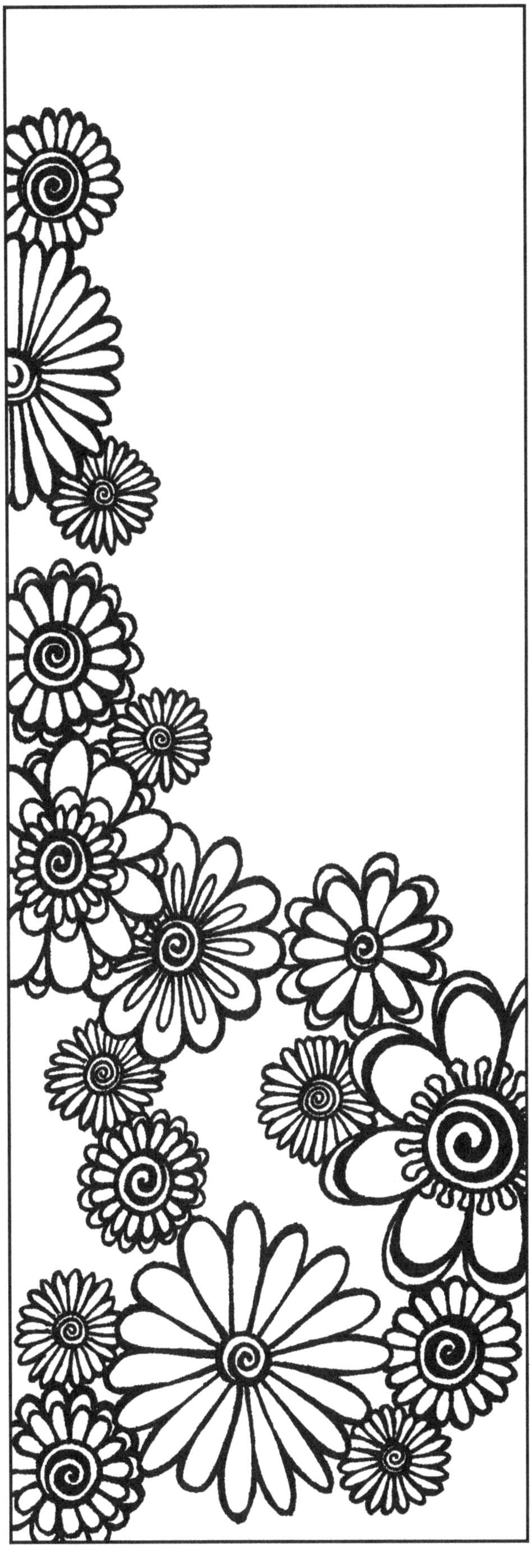

Color Test Page

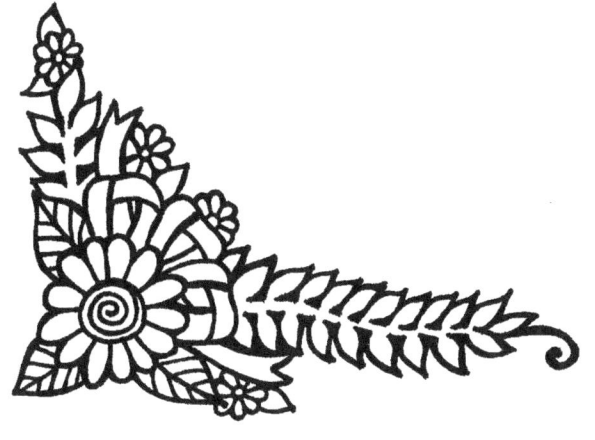

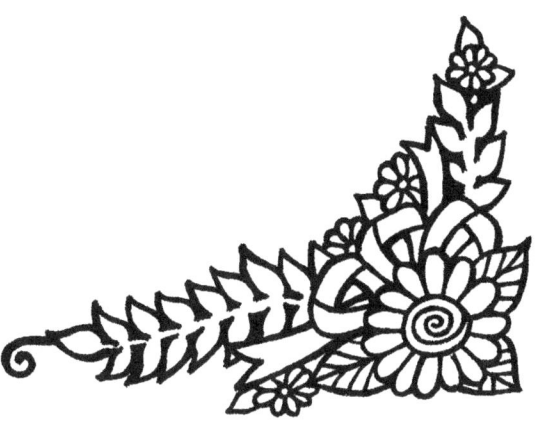

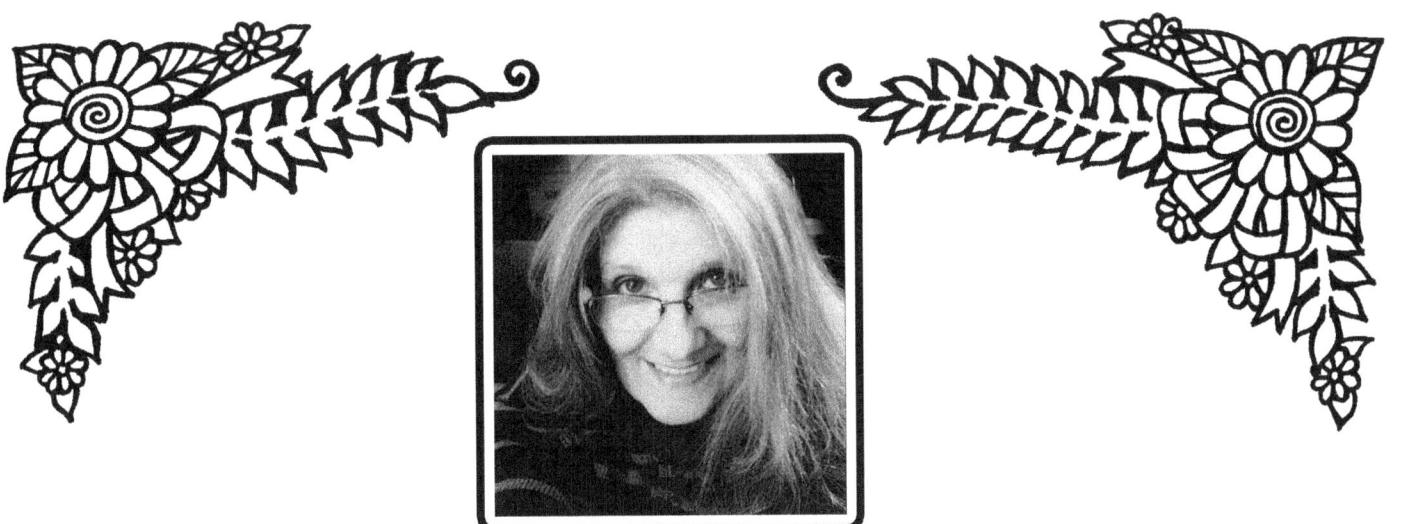

I'm a freelance Illustrator who has always felt a special connection to and love for nature. I've always been drawn to the ornate detail and complexity found throughout nature whether it be in the structured patterns of pine cones, the beautiful stained glass look of dragonfly and butterfly wings, or the unique leaf and petal arrangements seen in plants and flowers. I love doing ornate pen and ink nature themed artwork. Most of them start out as detailed hand drawn pencil sketches or illustrations. I enjoy adding intricate details and hidden "treasures" in my inky nature designs.

I've turned some of my nature themed art into digital designs and made them available on clothing and apparel in my online stores . I've been a working illustrator in the apparel industry for the last five years where I've been designing artwork for clothing and other merchandise as "OfficeInk Designs". As "OfficeInk" my designs have been featured online at Teefury, Ript Apparel, Shirt.Woot, ShirtPunch, Design By Humans, Redbubble, Society6, Etsy, and in my new online Amazon store as OfficeInk Designs.

Many times over the years fans and followers have approached me and suggested or requested my inky line work from designs be made available as color sheets or as an adult coloring book. So, for several years now I've been working on a series or adult coloring books in various themes, this being one of those books. I'm so pleased to see my collection of Inky ZenTangle styled Nature Designs become my new "Blossoms and Bugs" adult coloring and activity book and I'm so thrilled to finally be able to offer Blossoms and Bugs to the world.

AmedaNowlin.com

www.ingramcontent.com/pod-product-compliance
Lightning Source LLC
Chambersburg PA
CBHW060539210526
45170CB00019B/2114